普通高校"十二五"规划教材
国际经济与贸易系列

国际商务谈判

刘　莉　主　编
苏振东　副主编

清华大学出版社
北　京

内 容 简 介

本书包括11个方面的内容：国际商务谈判概述；国际商务谈判文化与礼仪；谈判的准备阶段；价格的谈判：询价；价格的谈判：报盘和还盘；订货；付款条件的谈判；包装的谈判；保险的谈判；装运的谈判和谈判策略。通过学习本书，学生能够初步掌握国际商务谈判的基本理论、实务知识和基本操作技能。

本书可作为普通高等院校相关专业课程的教材，也可作为相关工作人员的参考和培训用书。

图书在版编目（CIP）数据

国际商务谈判/刘莉主编. —北京：清华大学出版社，2014

（普通高校"十二五"规划教材 · 国际经济与贸易系列）

ISBN 978-7-302-34694-4

Ⅰ. ①国…　Ⅱ. ①刘…　Ⅲ. ①国际商务－商务谈判－高等学校－教材　Ⅳ. ①F740.41

中国版本图书馆CIP数据核字（2013）第290844号

责任编辑： 张　伟
封面设计： 汉风唐韵
责任校对： 王荣静
责任印制： 宋　林

出版发行： 清华大学出版社

网　　址： http://www.tup.com.cn，http://www.wqbook.com
地　　址： 北京清华大学学研大厦A座　　**邮　　编：** 100084
社 总 机： 010-62770175　　**邮　　购：** 010-62786544
投稿与读者服务： 010-62776969，c-service@tup.tsinghua.edu.cn
质量反馈： 010-62772015，zhiliang@tup.tsinghua.edu.cn
课件下载： http://www.tup.com.cn，010-62770177-4506

印 刷 者： 北京富博印刷有限公司
装 订 者： 北京市密云县京文制本装订厂
经　　销： 全国新华书店
开　　本： 185mm×230mm　　**印　张：** 9　　**字　　数：** 174千字
版　　次： 2014年1月第1版　　**印　　次：** 2014年1月第1次印刷
印　　数： 1～4000
定　　价： 19.00元

产品编号：047295-01

前言

本书依照教育部认真贯彻《国务院关于大力推进职业教育改革与发展的决定》要求，根据商务部最新制定的国际商务专业教学大纲的要求，针对学生的学习目标和职业操作能力的培养目标，对谈判流程进行详细的讲解，力求内容新颖，通俗易懂，强调实务的可操作性，便于学生学习，达到学以致用、活学活用，在实际国际商务谈判业务中将所学的理论知识和操作技能有机地结合起来。

本书以国际商务谈判为主线，以合同为中心，以国际谈判各个阶段为依据，详细地介绍了国际贸易实务知识。每章开头都有学习目标、学习重点，每章结束时有谈判案例及技能实训，实现了理论与技能相结合，具有较强的针对性、实用性、规范性和操作性。

通过本课程的学习，学生将在以下两个方面取得明显的收获。

(1) 了解国际商务谈判基本流程，形成对商务谈判流程的基本认识，从而建立对国际商务谈判基本知识框架的把握。

(2) 结合课后练习，更重视理论与实践的结合，进一步培养和提高提出问题、分析问题和解决问题的能力。

免费提供电子课件和习题答案，可以作为高校金融学和国际贸易专业本科生的专业教材，也可作为研究生和专科生的选用教材。

编者

2013 年 8 月

目录

Chapter 1 Fundamentals of International Business Negotiations

第 1 章 国际商务谈判概述

Lead-in

Negotiation as a significant social activity is a means of dealing with human relationships and resolving conflicts. It is also regarded as a product of social competition. With the international trade becoming more and more widespread, business negotiation skills have been fundamental for every college student.

Learning Objectives

In this chapter, you will be able to:

- Learn the concepts and principles of business negotiations.
- Know the stages of negotiations.

1.1 Concepts and Principles of Business Negotiation

People negotiate all the time, at work, at home, and as consumers. Since the development of human languages, there have been negotiations made amongst humans. As a significant social activity, negotiation is a means of dealing with human relationships and resolving conflicts and has never stopped.

In this book, the term negotiation refers to win-win situations such as those that occur when parties are trying to find a mutually acceptable solution to a complex conflict. Negotiation is a very complex social process. Many factors that shape a negotiation result do not occur during the negotiation. They occur before the parties start to negotiate, or shape the context around the negotiation.

A negotiation is one of the most common approaches used to make decisions and manage disputes. It is also the major building block for many other alternative dispute resolution procedures[1]. It is a problem-solving process in which two or more people voluntarily discuss their differences and attempt to reach an agreement on their common concerns, requiring participants to identify issues about what they differ, inform each other about their needs and interests, generate possible settlement options and bargain over the terms of the final agreement.[2] International business negotiations are made between business parties from different countries or regions in the hope of a successful transaction.

According to Dr. Nierenberg, "perfect" negotiations vividly manifests the following "fundamental principles" of negotiations.

Firstly, "negotiation" is an element of human behavior. It depends on communication, that is, it occurs between individuals. Whenever people exchange ideas with the intention of changing relationships, and whenever they hope to reach an agreement, they are negotiating. Secondly, "negotiations" take place only over issues that are "negotiable". Thirdly, "negotiations" take place only between people who have the same interest. Fourthly, "negotiations" take place only when negotiators are interested not only in taking but also in giving, and finally, "negotiations" take place only when negotiating parties trust each other.

1.2 The Stages of Negotiations

The process of international business negotiations can be divided into three different stages, the pre-negotiation stage, the negotiation stage and the post-negotiation stage. A stage refers to a specific part of the process and includes all actions and communications by any party pertaining to negotiations made during that part.

1. The Pre-negotiation Stage

The pre-negotiation stage begins with the first contact between parties in which an interest in doing business with each other is shown. During this stage, some negotiations take place. The dynamism of the process can be observed at this early stage where parties begin to understand each other's needs and evaluate the benefits of entering into the process of negotiations.[3]

The parties gather as much relevant information as possible about each other—the operating environment, the involvement of other third parties, influences, competitors and the infrastructure.[4]

During this stage, the parties can openly talk about objectives and expectations. They can also have informal meetings to examine each other's situation. Trust and confidence gained from these relationships increase the chances of agreement. After this step, parties begin to formulate their strategy for face-to-face negotiations, including comparing the alternatives available, deciding on possible points of concession, foreseeing predictable events. Finally, it is necessary to understand the infrastructure of the country and the company.

For the initial strategy, the negotiators should list the problems and issues, especially the conflicting issues and form strategies and choices for all possible solutions they or the other party could suggest.

2. The Face-to-face Negotiation Stage

At this stage, two parties come together to find a solution to a joint problem. Both parties have different angles and interests, therefore, each of them should have an open mind and prepare for several alternatives. As the process continues, the parties should evaluate the alternatives presented by the other party and select those that are compatible with their own expectations.[5]

3. The Post-negotiation Stage

At this stage, all the terms have been agreed upon. The contract is being drawn up and is ready to be signed. Because of differences in values and customs among different countries, in cases involving Western companies and emerging-country parties, the language used and the recording of issues previously agreed upon take a large amount of time.[6]

Notes

(1) It is also the major building block for many other alternative dispute resolution procedures.

谈判也是解决其他许多争端程序中的一个重要解决办法。

(2) It is a problem-solving process in which two or more people voluntarily discuss their differences and attempt to reach a joint decision on their common concerns, requiring participants to identify issues about what they differ, inform each other about their needs and interests, generate possible settlement options and bargain over the terms of the final agreement.

这是一个解决问题的过程。在此过程中,双方或更多方自愿讨论之间的分歧,试图就共同关注的问题做出共同决定。这就要求有关各方辨别出彼此的不同,将彼此的利益需求告知对方,提出可行的解决方法,在讨价还价中达成最终共识。

(3) The dynamism of the process can be observed at this early stage where parties begin to understand each other's needs and evaluate the benefits of entering into the process of negotiations.

这个初始阶段的进展会比较积极,因为双方会开始了解对方的需求,估测己方参加谈判的好处。

(4) The parties gather as much relevant information as possible about each other—the operating environment, the involvement of other third parties, influences, competitors and the infrastructure.

双方会尽可能地搜集有关对方的信息,如运营环境、第三方的参与、影响因素、竞争对手和基础设施等。

(5) As the process continues, the parties should evaluate the alternatives presented by the other party and select those that are compatible with their own expectations.

随着谈判的推进,谈判方应评估对方提出的备选方案,从中选出与己方预期一致的方案来。

(6) Because of difference in values and customs among different countries, in cases involving Western companies and emerging-country parties, the language used and the recording of issues previously agreed upon take a large amount of time.

由于不同的国家有不同的价值观和风俗，在一些涉及西方企业与新兴国家市场合作的谈判中,双方会用相当长的时间就措辞及已达成共识的文字记载进行确认。

Case Study

What is Your Walk-away Price?

In any business negotiation you must start by determining your "walk-away" price—the top price you are willing to pay when the final price is discussed. The walk-away price should not include the full potential value of the synergies of the deal. Why? The synergies are possible additional positive outcomes that may happen—but they are not part of the deal and thus should not influence your negotiation or walk-away price. In addition, for a walk-away price to be real—and it is a critical part of any negotiation—you must be ready to walk away.

For example, when Carlos Gutierrez, CEO of Kellogg Company, the cereal giant, was negotiating the purchase of Keebler, the cookie company, he was most eager to close the deal.

Keebler had a direct-to-buyer delivery system that enabled it to carry products to stores in its own trucks, by passing the retailers' warehouses altogether, which Gutierrez viewed as an enormous synergistic benefit of acquiring Keebler. However, his staff had calculated that at maximum Keebler was worth $42 a share—less than Keebler negotiators would accept. In similar situations, the staff who established the walk-away price consisted of a decision-making group of highly trusted senior managers given veto power over the final number. They were not concerned with synergies, but with the goal of establishing a balanced, objective estimation of the facts.

In the final bargaining session Gutierrez told Keebler's management that $42 was his walk-away price—and left to watch a Mets baseball game and forget the deal. Two days later, after Gutierrez made it clear that he had made his final offer, Keebler accepted the $42 BATNA offer, the best alternative to a negotiated agreement.

The next time you begin a negotiation, ask yourself—or better yet, ask other trusted individuals: What is your walk-away price? Write it down and stick to it.

(Geoffrey Cullinan, Jean-Marc Le Roux, Rolf-Magnus Weddigen. When to Walk Away from a Deal[J]. Harvard Business Review, 2004(4): 96-104.)

Negotiation Examples

1

(A potential[1] foreign investor, who is new to the Chinese market, is making inquiries about[2] the possibility of setting up joint ventures in China.)

A = Foreigner B = Chinese

A: Mr. Zhao, I'd like to have your expert advice[3]. You see, I've been contemplating[4] making an investment in China. What kinds of foreign operations are allowed in your country?

B: Well, I can't say I'm an expert in this field. But I certainly can tell you something about foreign direct investments in China. Foreign investments are welcome in priority industries[5]. Tax incentives and other preferential treatments[6] are available at local and industrial levels.

A: So the government policy is to encourage foreign investments, isn't it? Are there any screening criteria[7]?

B: Yes, there are.

A: In which industries are foreign participation and involvement encouraged or permitted or even prohibited?

B: Foreign participation and ownership are encouraged in priority sectors in terms of industry, and in export-oriented and technologically advanced projects[8]. Restrictions are placed on the foreign involvements in certain industries, such as retailing and media. To help investors, the Chinese government has adopted many new measures recently to create a more favorable investment environment[9].

A: And what are the possible business structures or entities[10] by which foreigners can operate in China?

B: Well, China allows various forms of foreign investments, including Sino-foreign joint ventures and wholly foreign-owned enterprises[11]. The forms of foreign investments in China are barter trade, compensation trade, processing arrangements[12], joint ventures, including equity joint ventures, cooperative joint ventures, and wholly foreign-owned enterprises. Foreign companies may also set up representative offices for liaison purposes[13].

A: I'm interested in the business structure of Sino-foreign joint ventures. You have mentioned two types of joint ventures: cooperative joint ventures and equity joint ventures[14]. So what is the difference between them?

B: First, in an equity joint venture, profit distributions and management responsibilities are determined by the proportion of total registered capital contributed by each party[15].

A: So profits are distributed according to each partner's investment ratio.

B: That's right. The cooperative joint venture, which is also referred to as a contractual joint venture, however, is an investment vehicle in which profits and other responsibilities are assigned to each party according to the joint venture contract.

A: In other words, profit distributions among partners in a cooperative joint venture need not be in strict proportion to their registered capital contribution[16].

B: Exactly. Thank you for your interest in us. The projects you've just proposed are interesting. But we don't have time to go into details today. Can we meet again tomorrow?

Notes

(1) potential：潜在的

(2) making inquiries about：咨询、询问、查询

(3) expert advice：专家的意见，行家的建议

(4) contemplate：考虑、思考

(5) priority industries：重点产业

(6) tax incentives and other preferential treatments：税收减免和其他优惠待遇

(7) screening criteria：审批标准

(8) in priority sectors in terms of industry, and in export-oriented and technologically advanced projects: 在优先发展的产业部门,出口导向型和技术先进的项目

(9) adopt many new measures recently to create a more favorable investment environment: 近来采取措施创造良好的投资环境

(10) possible business structures or entities: 可能的企业组织形式或实体

(11) Sino-foreign joint ventures and wholly foreign-owned enterprises: 中外合资企业和外商独资企业

(12) barter trade, compensation trade, processing arrangements: 易货贸易、补偿贸易、加工贸易

(13) representative offices for liaison purposes: 旨在开展联络的代表处

(14) cooperative joint venture and equity joint venture: 合作企业和股权合资企业

(15) Profit distributions and management responsibilities are determined by the proportion of total registered capital contributed by each party.

合资企业的利润分配和管理分工是由投资各方在注册资本中所占的比例决定的。

(16) need not be in strict proportion to their registered capital contribution: 不必严格按照投资各方出资的多少

2

A: Mr. Li, I know it is critical[1] to expand into new markets or enter into new fields[2] of business activities. But what sort of information should I look for?

B: First, you need to find out whether there is any demand for your products and what competition[3] you will meet. Then you have to know about the local conditions and preferences[4], that is, the government regulations, business customs and practices, and cultural background[5].

A: That's true. Among different customers in markets, there is a wide variety of taste, customs, behaviors and expectations[6]. Then how can we acquire[7] all the necessary information about a new market and a new customer[8]?

B: It can be obtained through various channels[9]. You can have access to Internet[10] to search for valuable information.

A: Are there any official organizations[11] which can provide me with information about new markets and potential customers?

B: Yes. Banks, Chamber of Commerce and Commercial Counselors' Offices[12] can be helpful in building business relationships. They can also give you advice about the size of markets, their location and price sensitivity as well as import controls in specific areas[13].

A：Can I get some information from the newspapers and magazines?

B：Yes，you might also get information from some trade and publications and magazines. They have financial data about the volume and value of specific products exported to and imported from any single country in the world. They will help you compare specifications，functions，quality and packaging of products[14].

A：We plan to go global[15]. Then how should we enter overseas markets in the first place?

B：You may use an intermediary[16]，such as an export agent，to deal with buyers in the overseas market.

A：Can we have direct exports?

B：Yes，you can handle your own exports by setting up overseas sales offices. You can also sell the rights to use a manufacturing process，trademark or patent for a fee or royalty[17].

A：Can we work together with a local firm to develop a particular market?

B：Sure. You can establish a joint venture[18] in China with a local firm. You can also buy a local company，or set up your own manufacturing subsidiaries[19].

Notes

(1) critical：重要的，关键的

(2) expand into new markets or enter into new fields：开发新市场、进入新领域

(3) competition：竞争

(4) local conditions and preferences：当地的市场状况以及喜好

(5) the government regulations，business customs and practices，and cultural background：政府的规章制度、经商习惯、商业实际和文化背景

(6) there is a wide variety of taste，customs，behaviors and expectations：在顾客的品位、风俗习惯、购买行为以及顾客的期望值方面有很多差异

(7) acquire：获得

(8) customer：顾客

(9) obtained through various channels：通过各种渠道收集

(10) have access to Internet：上网

(11) official organizations：官方组织

(12) Chamber of Commerce and Commercial Counselors' Office：商会、商务咨询处

(13) advice about the size of markets，their location and price sensitivity as well as import controls in specific areas：市场的大小、方位、价格的敏感度以及进口限制等许多有用的信息

(14) compare specifications，functions，quality and packaging of products：对产品的规

格、用途、质量、包装和外观做比较

(15) We plan to go global: 我公司打算向国外扩展

(16) intermediary: 代理商

(17) sell the rights to use a manufacturing process, trademark or patent for a fee or royalty: 出售生产技术、商标、专利

(18) joint ventures: 合资企业

(19) set up your own manufacturing subsidiaries: 设立分公司

Word Bank

business scope/frame 经营范围
trade by commodities 商品贸易
visible trade 有形贸易
invisible trade 无形贸易
barter trade 易货贸易
bilateral trade 双边贸易
triangle trade 三角贸易
multilateral trade 多边贸易
counter trade 对销贸易;抵偿贸易
compensation trade 补偿贸易
processing trade 来料加工贸易
assembling trade 来料装配贸易
leasing trade 租赁贸易
to establish/enter into/set up a business relationship 建立业务关系
to continue a business relationship 继续业务关系
to present a business relationship 保持业务关系
to improve a business relationship 改善业务关系
to promote a business relationship 促进业务关系
to speed up a business relationship 加快业务关系的发展
to enlarge/widen a business relationship 扩大业务关系
to restore/resume a business relationship 恢复业务关系
to interrupt a business relationship 中断业务关系
to cement a business relationship 巩固业务关系

Useful Sentences

(1) Business negotiations are a delicate matter.

商务谈判是一件十分微妙的事情。

(2) Tom has good interpersonal and communication skills, and is able to negotiate with business partners.

汤姆的人际沟通能力强,能进行商务谈判。

(3) Cooperative manners are an important part of international business negotiations.

合作礼仪是国际商务谈判的重要组成部分。

(4) I have an important business negotiation with a company in Shanghai.

我与上海一家公司有一个重要的商务谈判。

(5) To work in our company, you need to have good business negotiation and communication abilities.

作为我们公司的员工,你需要有良好的商务谈判能力及沟通能力。

(6) The success of international business relationships depends on effective business negotiations.

国际商务关系的成功建立取决于有效的商务谈判。

(7) As for the leader of our group, he is hardworking and responsible with good ability of sales management and business negotiations.

至于我们团队的负责人,他勤奋负责,具有较强的销售管理能力、商务谈判能力。

(8) The cultural differences often cause misunderstanding and arguments that lead to a total failure in business negotiations.

文化差异导致的误解和争执,竟会导致商务谈判失败。

(9) Therefore, having a basic knowledge of business and trade terminology in English is helpful in actual business negotiations.

因此懂得一些商务和贸易的英语术语对实际的商务谈判是非常有用的。

(10) They can both negotiate and communicate well with oversea customers independently.

他们能独立跟国外客户进行很好的商务谈判和沟通。

(11) They would not believe the first quotation of the other party in the commercial negotiations.

在商务谈判中,他们一般不会相信对方的第一次报价。

(12) As the manager, he conducts TAC (Total Acquisition Cost) analysis and leads the commercial negotiations with potential suppliers.

作为经理,他进行整体采购成本分析,领导与潜在供应商进行的商务谈判。

(13) A commercial negotiation is a science, also an art. It is nearly ubiquitous in the economic life.

商务谈判是一门科学,又是一门艺术,在经济生活中几乎无处不在。

(14) Now I will tell you some simple negotiation rites, teach you some techniques with successful alignments.

现在我来告诉大家一些简单的谈判礼仪,教大家一些走向成功的技巧。

(15) A good negotiator should grasp communication and presentation skills, problem-solving techniques, being able to deal with unexpected negotiation situations.

一个优秀的谈判者应该掌握良好的沟通和表述能力以及解决问题的技巧,能够应对意料之外的谈判局面。

Tactics for Success

Use Time to Your Advantage

(1) Have patience. Because most concessions and settlements occur in the last 20% of the available time, remain level-headed and wait for the right moment to act. As a general rule, patience pays.

(2) Be persistent. Your counterpart is most likely not going to concede to your needs and desires at the beginning of the negotiation. If your first request does not work, try a different frame, or provide additional information that might persuade your counterpart to make a concession. Don't give up on your first try. Patience and persistence pay off in negotiations.

(3) Move quickly when possible. There will be times when one or both parties will benefit if negotiations are resolved quickly. If this is the case, sell your counterpart on the benefits to him of a speedy resolution.

(4) Realize that deadlines can be moved, changed or eliminated. As your deadline comes near, do not panic. You can change it! Have you ever wondered why so many people run to the post office to file their tax returns at the last minute on April 15 when they could easily file an extension, gaining another four months or more to send in their forms?

(5) Know your counterpart's timeline. In most negotiations, you are better off if you know your counterpart's deadline and she does not know yours. As you come near her deadline, your counterpart's stress level will increase, and she will be more likely to make concessions.

(6) Make time work for you. As a rule, you will not achieve the best outcome quickly. Although there are some exceptions, you will usually be better off moving slowly and with perseverance, even if it means changing your deadline.

(Peter B Stark, Jane Flaherty. The Only Negotiating Guide You'll Ever Need[M]. New York: Broadway Books, 2003:20.)

Exercises

Ⅰ. Translate the following words and phrases

put it simply
market research
coupon
strength
mass consumption products
a steady demand
enjoy a good reputation
prospective buyer
handle various kinds of products
give priority to
贸易协会
贸易展销会
贸易前景
贸易界
符合你们的要求
超过其他公司
合作范围
供应商
管理经验
原料

Ⅱ. Translate the following sentences

(1) The purpose of the negotiation is to arrive at an agreement to both sides' advantages.

(2) The successful results of the negotiations depend on the determined objectives, perseverance and the language expressed by the negotiators.

(3) They should do their best to use soft words, use less flowery language, have a sense of humor and create a harmonious atmosphere.

(4) 国际商务谈判是发生在政府之间、贸易组织之间、跨国公司之间、私人商业组织之间和买卖双方之间的关于投资、商品进出口、机械设备进出口以及技术进出口的一个磋商过程。

(5) 谈判是全面完成进出口贸易协定的重要步骤之一。

Do You Know

Ten Best Practices for Negotiators

(1) Best prepared.

(2) Diagnose the fundamental structure of the negotiation.

(3) Identify and work the BATNA (the best alternative to a negotiated agreement).

(4) Be willing to walk away.

(5) Master paradoxes.

(6) Remember the intangibles.

(7) Actively manage coalitions.

(8) Savor and protect your reputation.

(9) Remember that rationality and fairness are relative.

(10) Continue to learn from the experience.

(Roy J Lewicki, Bruce Barry, David M Saunders. 谈判学精要[M]. 大连：东北财经大学出版社，2008.)

Chapter 2 Business Culture and Etiquette in Negotiations

第 2 章　国际商务谈判文化与礼仪

Lead-in

People from different countries have different values, attitudes and experiences. Therefore, to understand the cultural difference is the key in business negotiations. We also need to respect the etiquette special in some cultures so as to achieve successes in international business.

Learning Objectives

In this chapter, you will be able to:

- Learn the cultural differences between different countries.
- Understand the global business protocol and etiquette.

Nowadays, the world is developing quickly in the age of economic globalization.[1] Under this circumstance, opportunities for international business negotiations are on a dramatic increase. Negotiators from different countries conduct business in different ways, which are influenced by their cultures.[2] Thus, international negotiators tend to act according to their own values shaped by culture. Culture can influence language, beliefs, and behaviors and negotiating styles in numerous ways.[3] When the two parties from different cultures at the negotiating table pursue their own interests respectively, problems often crop up leading to misunderstanding between them.[4] Discussions are frequently hindered because of different communication styles. Even though negotiators are technologically well prepared, it is not easy to reach a satisfactory agreement between negotiators across cultures.[5] Understandings of the issues in negotiations vary from culture to culture. According to Moran (1991), there are two basic concepts of negotiations: strategic and synergistic.[6] Americans tend to be strategic while Japanese are synergistic. Americans see negotiations as a competitive process while a collaborative exercise for Japanese.[7] Americans negotiate a contract while Japanese negotiate a personal relationship.[8] By understanding the counterpart's styles of negotiations, negotiators can make appropriate strategies to arrive at an agreement.[9]

To be fully prepared for a negotiation, negotiators should pay attention to the cultural differences such as privacy, time, dinner etiquette, and so on.[10] These elements will directly or indirectly influence the process and effects of negotiations.

1. Privacy

Generally speaking, Chinese people have relatively weak concepts about privacy. They tend to emphasize unity and friendship. Chinese people are willing to understand other people's feelings. However, privacy is very important for Westerners who emphasize personal space and are not willing to mention much about their own affairs. So it is impolite to ask about the foreigners' age, marital status, incomes and so on.

2. Time

In Westerners' eyes, "time is money" and they treasure every minute. Therefore, they try to have careful arrangements and work efficiently. They tend to carefully plan every stage of the itinerary before their visit. Chinese people may believe it a hospitable action to invite others to a dinner in the hope of facilitating the negotiations. However, Westerners may not take it as equally important.

3. Dinner Etiquettes

China has been called the nation of hospitality. On some occasions, some Chinese people may give their cigarettes to each other. At a Chinese banquet, there may be a lot of dishes on the table. The host may use chopsticks to help guests get some food, and persuade guests to drink and eat more. In Western countries, however, people stress respect for individuals' rights and privacy, and therefore they will give guests the freedom to choose what they want.

Thinking styles between Western and Eastern people are different, which shapes different styles of negotiations.[11] In the West, logics, analysis and precision are emphasized while in the East, intuition and feelings are stressed.[12] Western people are direct and specific while Eastern people are indirect, vague and general.[13] For instance, Americans tend to see the goal of negotiations as to lead to a binding contract, which creates rights and obligations.[14] But Japanese may see the goal of negotiations as to create a relationship between the two parties, and the written contract is an expression of that relationship. The Japanese believe that the willingness to modify a contract reflects changes in the parties relationship[15] while Americans see it as a tendency to renege and insist on adhering to the original terms of the contract.[16]

All in all, to be an effective negotiator, one should recognize and accept the differences, respect each other's culture, and understand how culture shapes the goals and strategic preferences.[17] It is crucial to resolve such cultural conflicts so that negotiators can reach an agreement through effective negotiations.

Notes

(1) Nowadays, the world is developing quickly in the age of economic globalization.

当今,世界在经济一体化的时代飞速发展。

(2) Negotiators from different countries conduct business in different ways, which are influenced by their cultures.

不同国家的谈判者以不同的方式做生意,这些方式都受到他们文化的影响。

(3) Culture can influence language, beliefs, and behaviors and negotiating styles in numerous ways.

文化会影响语言、信念、行为,并在许多方面影响着谈判风格。

(4) When the two parties from different culture sat the negotiating table pursue their own interests respectively, problems often crop up leading to misunderstanding between them.

当文化不同的双方在谈判桌前追求各自的利益时,很容易出现问题,导致双方的误解。

(5) Even though negotiators are technologically well prepared, it is not easy to reach a satisfactory agreement between negotiators across cultures.

尽管从技术层面来讲,谈判者已经准备好了,但要想在不同文化的谈判者之间达成令人满意的协议还是不容易。

(6) there are two basic concepts of negotiations: strategic and synergistic.

对于谈判有两种认识:策略性的和相互促进性的。

(7) Americans see negotiations as a competitive process while a collaborative exercise for

Japanese.

美国人把谈判看成是竞争的过程,而日本人把谈判看成是合作的过程。

(8) Americans negotiate a contract; Japanese negotiate a personal relationship.

美国人通过谈判签订合同;日本人通过谈判建立个人关系。

(9) By understanding the counterpart's styles of negotiations, negotiators can make appropriate strategies to arrive at an agreement.

通过了解对方的谈判风格,谈判者可以实行恰当的策略来达成协议。

(10) To be fully prepared for the negotiation, negotiators should pay attention to the cultural differences such as privacy, time, dinner etiquette, and so on.

要为谈判做好充分的准备,谈判者要对于个人隐私、时间观念、餐桌礼仪等文化差异加以关注。

(11) Thinking styles between Western and Eastern people are different, which shapes different styles of negotiations.

东西方思维方式的不同导致了谈判风格的不同。

(12) In the West, logics, analysis and precision are emphasized while in the East, intuition and feelings are stressed.

在西方,强调逻辑、分析和精确;在东方,强调直觉和感情。

(13) Western people are direct and specific while Eastern people are indirect, vague and general.

西方人的风格是直接、具体,东方人的风格是间接、模糊、宽泛。

(14) Americans tend to see the goal of negotiations as to lead to a binding contract, which creates rights and obligations.

美国人认为谈判的目标是达成一份合约,合约产生权利和义务。

(15) The Japanese believe that the willingness to modify a contract reflects changes in the parties relationship.

日本人认为修改合同的意愿反映出双方关系中的变化。

(16) Americans see it as a tendency to renege and insist on adhering to the original terms of the contract.

美国人把它看做意图违约,并坚持遵守合同中的原始条款。

(17) All in all, to be an effective negotiator, one should recognize and accept the differences, respect each other's culture, and understand how culture shapes the goals and strategic preferences.

总而言之,要做一个高效的谈判高手,就要认识和接受各自的差异,尊重彼此的文化,弄清文化是如何影响谈判目标和策略偏好的。

Traps to Avoid

The Nibble

The nibble occurs when negotiators reach agreement on all of the major issues—but then, as they prepare to close the deal, one side proposes a small concession on "one last" item, which they claim is needed to close the deal. For example, in a common new car purchase situation, the nibble may come after the price and all other issues have been agreed to, and the buyer sits down with the dealer's financial representative, who then suggests such nibbles as an extended warranty, undercoating, dealer prep or delivery charges. The buyer should understand these are all high-profit-margin items that add to the price of the car. Often the correct response to nibbles is a firm, but polite "No, thank you" because in reality the other party does not need this last item to close the deal.

(Peter B Stark, Jane Flaherty. The Only Negotiating Guide You'll Ever Need[M]. New York: Broadway Books, 2003:170.)

Negotiation Examples

1

A: Good morning, Angela. Can you spare me some time to talk?

B: Sure. You look terrible today.

A: Yeah. I have been very busy recently preparing for my negotiation with an export company from Belgium and I feel very exhausted.

B: What can I do to help you to relieve your pressure?

A: I hear that you have done business with Belgium. Can you give me some information about its economy?

B: Well. Belgium has capitalized on its central geographic location, highly developed its transport networks and diversified industrial and commercial products. Its industry is concentrated mainly in the populous Flemish area in the north[1].

A: It is said that its economy unusually depends on the state of world markets[2], right?

B: Yes. With few natural resources, Belgium must import substantial quantities of raw materials and export a large volume of manufactured products[3].

A: I have searched the Internet and found that about three-quarters of its business is done with other EU countries.

B: Belgium, together with its EU partners, began circulating euro currency in January 2002 and the government has succeeded in balancing its budget[4].

A: So what should I prepare in order to negotiate successfully if I visit Belgium?

B: There are several suggestions for you. Ideally, business cards should be printed in French or Flemish on the reverse side, depending on the main language of the region you visit[5].

A: Good idea. I will ask my secretary to take charge of it today.

B: An important thing you should bear in mind is that Belgium's cultural and linguistic divisions are a particularly sensitive subject[6]. So you should make an effort not to confuse the three cultural groups and their languages.

A: OK. I will take notes after I search for the relevant information.

B: The third point is about religion. Most Belgians are Catholic and bi-or tri-lingual. Nevertheless, religious, linguistic and ethnic biases persist. For example, French speakers generally believe that they are of a higher class, while the Walloons feel superior to the Flemish[7].

A: Well, you are a very experienced negotiator.

B: The fourth one is that you need to make sure meetings go smooth without interruptions. Leaving a meeting to get a phone call, go to the toilet or for any other reasons will only be viewed with annoyance by your Belgian counterparts[8].

A: I hear that Belgians are receptive to "outside" ideas and concepts, is it true?

B: Yes. They are willing to compromise when necessary. If you do business with Flanders, decisions are made by the group. In Walloon, however, the business culture tends to be intensely hierarchical and only the highest person in authority makes the final decision[9].

Notes

(1) Industry is concentrated mainly in the populous Flemish area in the north.

工业主要集中在人口密集的北部佛兰德地区。

(2) It is said that its economy unusually depends on the state of world markets.

据说该地区的经济十分依赖世界市场的经济状况。

(3) With few natural resources, Belgium must import substantial quantities of raw materials and export a large volume of manufactured products.

由于自然资源匮乏,比利时必须进口大量的原材料,出口大量的加工产品。

(4) Belgium, together with its EU partners, began circulating euro currency in January 2002 and the government has succeeded in balancing its budget.

从 2002 年 1 月,欧元开始在比利时和其他欧盟国家流通,比利时政府也实现了收支平衡。

(5) Ideally, business cards should be printed in French or Flemish on the reverse side, depending on the main language of the region you visit.

名片的背面最好为法文或者佛兰德语,这取决于您要拜访地区所使用的语言。

(6) An important thing you should bear in mind is that Belgium's cultural and linguistic divisions are a particularly sensitive subject.

您要记住很重要的一点:比利时的文化和语言划分是个敏感的话题。

(7) French speakers generally believe that they are of a higher class, while the Walloons feel superior to the Flemish.

说法语的人通常认为自己比别人高人一等,而沃伦人觉得比佛兰德人优越。

(8) Leaving a meeting to get a phone call, go to the toilet or for any other reasons will only be viewed with annoyance by your Belgian counterparts.

开会中途离开去接电话,或去卫生间或出于其他原因,都是比利时人很反感的事情。

(9) In Walloon, however, the business culture tends to be intensely hierarchical and only the highest person in authority makes the final decision.

在沃伦,商业文化等级性极强,只有最具权威的人才能做最后的决定。

2

A: Hello, David. Last time we had the chance of doing business with a German company. You can not imagine that they had prepared for the negotiation so carefully that we seemed to have done nothing in advance. [1]

B: From my experience, they regard formality and use of surnames as signs of respect. [2] This can be found when you have correspondence with them. [3]

A: Truly, they are very slow at making decisions. If they have a consensus, it will take them a long time. [4]

B: They stick to the facts. In my opinion, if we negotiate with Germans, honesty is a good policy. [5] By the way, I hear that you have a French friend. Do you have some suggestions for my next negotiation with a French company?

A: France is a country of personal networks. So connections count heavily in this country. [6] Generally speaking, it is a good way to make an initial contact such as trade show and official trade promotion. [7] Or you can arrange a formal meeting with potential customers, distributors or partners. [8]

B: How important is the punctuality in France?

A: Well, punctuality is very critical.[9] People should be on time for business meetings. In France, people are verbally and nonverbally expressive. They love to argue, often engaging in spirited debate during business meetings. Can you give me some suggestions on how to deal with British people?

B: To tell you the truth, British people don't like exaggerations[10]. If you plan to do a presentation, it should be straight-forward and factual[11]. English negotiators have done business all over the world for hundreds of years. They may put a wide safety margin in their opening position so as to leave room for substantial concessions during the bargaining process[12]. This practice may put off negotiators from Germany. For their decision-making process, it is also time-consuming[13]. Before you sign the contract, you need to stress the legal aspects and check items of the written agreement carefully[14]. If there occurs a dispute or disagreement, the British are likely to rely on the terms of the contract.

A: Thank you very much. It is so good to share the experience with each other.

Notes

(1) You cannot imagine that they had prepared for the negotiation so carefully that we seemed to have done nothing in advance.

你无法想象他们对于谈判准备得如此仔细,以至我们看上去像是没有提前准备似的。

(2) From my experience, they regard formality and use of surnames as signs of respect.

从我的经验来讲,他们认为正式和使用姓氏是表示尊重的表现。

(3) This can be found when you have correspondence with them.

这在与他们通信的过程中可窥一斑。

(4) Truly, they are very slow at making decisions. If they have a consensus, it will take them a long time.

确实,他们做决定很慢。如果他们要达成一致,那需要花的时间很长。

(5) Honesty is a good policy.

诚实是个好策略。

(6) So connections count heavily in this country.

在这个国家,关系很重要。

(7) Usually, it is a good way to make an initial contact such as trade show and official trade promotion.

通常要采用贸易展览和正式的贸易促销作为最初的接触手段才好。

(8) Or you can arrange a formal meeting with potential customers, distributors or part-

ners.

或者你可以安排一次正式的与潜在客户、分销商和合作者的会面。

(9) punctuality is very critical.

准时很重要。

(10) To tell you the truth, British people don't like exaggerations.

告诉你吧，英国人不喜欢夸张。

(11) If you plan to do a presentation, it should be straight-forward and factual.

如果你做展示，一定要直接、切实。

(12) They may put a wide safety margin in their opening position so as to leave room for substantial concessions during the bargaining process.

他们可能在开始时留出足够的余地，这样在讨价还价时可以做出大幅度的让步。

(13) This practice may put off negotiators from Germany. For their decision-making process, it is also time-consuming.

这种做法可能会得罪德国人。至于他们的决策过程，时间要很长。

(14) Before you sign the contract, you need to stress the legal aspects and check items of the written agreement carefully.

在你签约以前，需要强调法律事宜，并仔细检查好文件的各个条款。

Word Bank

出口信贷　export credit
出口津贴　export subsidy
商品倾销　dumping
外汇倾销　exchange dumping
优惠关税　special preferences
保税仓库　bonded warehouse
贸易顺差　favorable balance of trade
贸易逆差　unfavorable balance of trade
进口配额制　import quotas
自由贸易区　free trade zone
对外贸易值　value of foreign trade
国际贸易值　value of international trade
普遍优惠制　generalized system of preferences-GSP
最惠国待遇　most-favored nation treatment-MFNT
国际贸易　international trade

国内贸易 domestic trade
沿海贸易 coasting trade
特惠贸易 preferential trade
易货贸易 barter trade
补偿贸易 compensation trade
违禁贸易 illicit trade
贸易壁垒 trade barriers
贸易顺差 surplus/favorable balance of trade
贸易逆差 deficit/unfavorable balance of trade
贸易惯例 trade practice
贸易远景 trade prospect/trade vistas
贸易风险 trade risk
贸易额 volume of transaction

Useful Sentences

(1) Angela is in charge of the contract and project negotiations and evaluates suppliers in terms of their services and delivery time etc..

安吉拉负责进行合同商务谈判、项目洽谈等,评估相关供应商的服务质量、交货时间。

(2) For the influence of culture on negotiation, we need to take the following aspects into consideration: protocol, time sensitivity and risk propensity.

至于文化差异对谈判的影响,我们要考虑以下方面:礼仪、时间观念和风险偏好。

(3) Although the basic elements of business negotiations are the same in any country, methods and techniques used to reach an agreement may not be the same for both parties.

虽然商务谈判的基本要素在任何国家都相同,但是对于双方而言达成合约的方法和技巧则不同。

(4) Certainly, any activity requiring accurate descriptions—legal proceedings, business discussions, and diplomatic negotiations—will still need expert translators.

当然,任何要求准确描述的活动诸如诉讼、商务谈判、外交谈判,都需要专家级的翻译人员。

(5) Business interpreters mainly serve the business circles in various business activities, such as business visits, talks, meetings and negotiations.

商务口译多用于与商务活动相关的场合,比如商务谈判、业务洽谈、商务合同签订仪式、商贸互访等。

(6) Mindsets influence ways of addressing issues, of collecting information, of choosing the relevant pieces of information and of assessing their "truthfulness", so that finally they influence the negotiation process and the resulting decisions.

思维影响到人们说话的方式、收集信息的方式、选择相关信息的方式、评估可信度的方式等,最终影响到谈判进程及相关决定。

(7) Chinese businessmen tend to have business negotiations in a rather indirect manner, as opposed to the direct manner of American businessmen.

中国人在商务谈判时倾向于使用一种迂回婉转的方式,而美国人则表现出一种直截了当的作风。

(8) For Americans to play a more effective role in international business negotiations, they must put forth more effort to improve their cross-cultural understanding.

美国人要在国际商务谈判中扮演更为有效的角色,他们就必须投入更多的努力提高跨文化的理解力。

(9) Good communication and coordination of business negotiations can help businesses cut costs, improve product quality, shorten delivery and increase their market competitiveness.

良好的沟通协调和商务谈判能力,能够帮助企业节约成本,提高产品质量,缩短交货期,增强市场竞争力。

(10) The decision-making process of Chinese companies is generally slow and time-consuming.

中国公司的决策过程通常耗时冗长。

(11) To reach the desired results, the negotiators must seriously carry out the trade policies of their own countries.

要想达到预期的谈判目的,谈判者必须认真地贯彻执行本国的外贸政策。

(12) Japanese place more emphasis on group harmony, consensus and the need to discuss proposals and actions.

日本人讲究把重点放在小组讨论上,在采纳建议和采取行动之前要进行讨论,达成一致。

(13) Etiquette usually reflects the formulas of conduct in which society or tradition has invested.

礼仪通常体现为社会或传统约定俗成的行为准则。

(14) A lot of Chinese avoid saying a clear "no" in order to save face for the others.

为了给别人留面子,很多中国人经常不明确地说一声"不"。

Tactics for Success

Nations and Regions Exhibiting Extremes in Hofstede's Cultural Dimensions

Low power distance Austria, Denmark, New Zealand, Israel, Ireland, U. S. A.	**High power distance** Malaysia, Philippines, Panama, Mexico, Venezuela
Low uncertainty avoidance Singapore, Denmark, Sweden, Hongkong, Jamaica, U. S. A.	**High uncertainty avoidance** Greece, Belgium, Portugal, Poland, Uruguay
Individualistic U. S. A., Australia, Great Britain, Netherlands, Canada, New Zealand	**Collectivist** Pakistan, Taipei, Indonesia, Costa Rica, Columbia, Japan
Masculinity Japan, Austria, Hungary, Venezuela, Italy, U. S. A.	**Feminist** Sweden, Norway, Netherlands, Denmark, Cost Rica
Low long-term orientation Canada, United Kingdom, U. S. A., Pakistan, Philippines	**High long-term orientation** Mainland China, Hongkong, Singapore, Japan, South Korea

A high power distance ranking indicates that inequalities of power and wealth have been allowed to grow within the society and that the ordering of people into a high or low place is "correct" and should be protected.

A high uncertainty avoidance ranking indicates that the society has a low tolerance for uncertainty and ambiguity.

A high individualism ranking indicates that individuality and individual rights are paramount within the culture.

A high masculinity ranking indicates that the society values achievement, control and power and has a high degree of gender differentiation.

A high long-term orientation ranking indicates that the society values long-term commitments and respect for tradition.

(Geert Hofstede. Culture's Consequences: International Differences in Work-Related Values[M]. Thousand Oaks: SAGE, 1984.)

Exercises

Ⅰ. Translate the following words and phrases

host country
prevailing values
frame the world views
legal system
formulas of conduct
proper salutation
content appropriate to the situation
subject line
superior-subordinate relationship
cross-cultural communication
领导风格
谈判过程
承担风险
交流风格
收集信息
决策过程
敏感话题
文化偏见
礼仪
风俗和传统

Ⅱ. Translate the following sentences

(1) In some cultures, people usually tolerate differences and uncertainty, whereas others do not stand these conditions.

(2) Cultures with high uncertainty avoidance always take security into consideration and tend to avoid conflict.

(3) Cultures with high uncertainty avoidance are quite comfortable with differences.

(4) 人们愿意冒险,对于不同的个人意见多有宽容,冲突往往被视作是建设性的,有益的,人们能够接受不同意见。

(5) 挪威和澳大利亚代表宽容文化的国家,日本和意大利则代表不宽容文化国家。

Do You Know

Clusters of Countries and Regions

(1) **Performance Orientation**: The degree to which a culture's people encourage and reward people for performance. (High: Germanic Europe, Confucian Asia and Anglo. Low: Eastern Europe and Latin America.)

(2) **In-Group Collectivism**: The degree to which a culture's people take pride in and feel loyalty toward their families, organizations and employers. (High: Southeast Asia, Confucian Asia, Eastern Europe and Middle East. Low: Anglo, Nordic Europe, and Germanic Europe.)

(3) **Institutional Collectivism**: The degree to which individuals are encouraged by institutions to be integrated into broader entities, with harmony and cooperation as paramount principles at the expense of autonomy and individual freedom. (High: Nordic Europe and Confucian Asia. Mid: Anglo. Low: Latin America, Germanic Europe and Latin Europe.)

(4) **Power Distance**: The degree to which a culture's people are separated by power, authority and prestige. (High: Southeast Asia, Eastern Europe and Latin America. Mid: Anglo and Confucian Asia. Low: Nordic Germany and Germanic Europe.)

(5) **Uncertainty Avoidance**: The degree to which a culture's people seek orderliness, consistency and structure. (High: Nordic Germany and Germanic Europe. Mid: Anglo and Confucian Asia. Low: Middle East, Eastern Europe and Latin America.)

(6) **Future Orientation**: The degree to which a culture's people are willing to defer immediate gratification for future benefits. (High: Germanic Europe and Nordic Europe. Mid: Anglo and Confucian Asia. Low: Middle East, Eastern Europe and Latin America.)

(7) **Gender Egalitarianism**: The degree to which a culture's people support gender equality. (High: Eastern Europe and Nordic Europe. Mid: Anglo and Confucian Asia. Low: Middle East and Germanic Europe.)

(8) **Assertiveness**: The degree to which a culture's people are assertive, confrontational, and aggressive. (High: Germanic Europe and Eastern Europe. Mid: Anglo and Confucian Asia. Low: Nordic Europe and Southeast Asia.)

(9) **Humane Orientation**: The degree to which a culture's people are fair, altruistic, generous, caring and kind toward others. (High: Southern Asia and Sub-Sahara Africa. Mid: Anglo and Confucian Asia. Low: Latin Europe and Germanic Europe.)

(Michael R Carrell, Christina Heavrin. Negotiating Essentials: Theory, Skills and Practices[M]. Upper Saddle River: Prentice Hall, 2010:228-229.)

Chapter 3 Preparing for Negotiation

第3章 谈判的准备阶段

Lead-in

A good negotiator will never ignore any preparation work which looks tiny but vital. Good preparation has an immediate impact on the opening stages of a negotiation, which sets the tone for the rest of the meetings.

Learning Objectives

In this chapter, you will be able to:

- Know how to schedule the first round of meeting.
- Prepare for negotiations.

For both parties, the first impression is very critical for the style, progress and eventual outcome of the negotiations.[1] Scheduling the first round of meetings is an important task for both parties and should be handled in a manner that preserves the professionalism of all the attendees.[2]

For the host, the choice of vehicles and hotels reflects a company's image and standing.[3] For the visitor, he should search the information about the local weather and traffic so that he can be dressed properly and be punctual at the meeting. Dinner manners, holidays, gift exchanges and religions should also be researched before the negotiation.

To achieve success in negotiation, there are several aspects to be considered: agenda, objectives, issues and positions, accommodation, meeting sites and physical environment. [4]

(1) Agenda: The visiting team needs to play an active role in designing the meeting agenda since maybe they will be responsible for the expenses related to it. [5] Experienced negotiators recognize that it works well for the host to abide by the agenda constructed by the visitors. The host must keep in mind that not all visitors view socializing as part of negotiations and that they may offend their guests with excessive hospitality. Visitors should also accommodate their host's wishes to be sociable, and do not keep agenda too tight. Agendas should be planned jointly ahead of arrival and schedules should be adhered to it as strictly as possible. [6] Moving smoothly from point to point in a timely fashion is far preferred.

An agenda may be presented by one party or prepared by both parties, or each party may prepare two agendas: a general agenda and a detailed agenda. The general agenda is presented to the other party, and the detailed agenda is for one's own use. The agenda should include items and assumptions, to reveal positions in advance and it may permit the other party to prepare a reaction to the areas that are wished for discussions. Many a negotiation has been circumscribed by an agenda based on a printed form or merely a chronological list of issues. Instead, both parties should pay attention to various issues to be discussed so that strategies can be developed. The issues might be listed so that the major ones are discussed first. This will prevent wasting time on minor issues and make sure of leaving sufficient time to discuss the major ones.

(2) Objectives: Any negotiation should be oriented by its objectives. The clear, specific, impersonal and feasible objectives will benefit the whole process of negotiation. [7] For the objectives, the following questions should be taken into consideration: Who can contribute to and who will be affected by the negotiation? Where is the best place for us to negotiate? What are the maximum and minimum targets we will seek? When must we conclude this negotiation and when would we like to conclude? How willing are we to make concessions and how will we seek counter-concessions from the other party? Why has the buyer selected us to negotiate with? Does this suggest any bargaining strengths for our side?

(3) Issues and positions: The issues are things on which the two parties disagree with each other. One party takes an affirmative position and the other a negative position. When the other party makes a commitment or sets a limit, one way of handling it would be to ignore it or not comprehend it or make a casual conversation or a joke. [8] Humor can serve a vital function in

negotiations. It is said that a bargaining position should conceal as well as reveal, and as negotiations continue, concessions alternate from each party. A motivating factor to cause such reactions is to cite principles and precedents for the other party to work with. [9]

(4) Accommodation, meeting site and physical environment: If the meeting is held in your own country, you have the following advantages: It prevents the other party from concluding the negotiation prematurely and leaving without notice, [10] which he might do if he is in his own office. You can take care of other matters and have your own facilities available while you are handling the negotiation. It gives you the psychological advantage of having the other party comes to you, and it saves you money and traveling time.

Visiting your counterpart's country also has advantages: you can devote your full time to the negotiation without distractions. You can withhold information, stating that it is not immediately available. You might have the option of going over your counterpart's head to someone in his higher management.

When either party chooses the accommodation places and meeting rooms, it shows the status of the company and the sincerity of negotiation. The party who arranges the meeting should take great efforts to assure a comfortable and relaxed atmosphere for reducing tension. It depends on the mood and style of negotiations whether negotiators should split into their respective teams or intermix either team. [11]

Notes

(1) For both parties, the first impression is very critical for the style, progress and eventual outcome of the negotiations.

对于谈判双方来说,第一印象对于谈判的风格、进度和最终的成败很关键。

(2) Scheduling the first round of meetings is an important task for both parties and should be handled in a manner that preserves the professionalism of all the attendees.

安排好第一轮的会议对双方都很重要,要以尊重所有与会人员的职业水准的方式来进行。

(3) For the host, the choice of vehicles and hotels reflects a company's image and standing.

对于主办方,交通工具和酒店的选择反映了该公司的形象和地位。

(4) To achieve success in negotiation, there are several aspects to be considered: agenda, objectives, issues and positions, accommodation, meeting sites and physical environment.

为了使得谈判顺利进行,有几个方面需要考虑:议程、目标、争议论题和立场、住宿、会议地点和环境。

(5) The visiting team needs to play an active role in designing the meeting agenda since maybe they will be responsible for the expenses related to it.

拜访方要积极设计议程,因为他们可能要为所产生的花销埋单。

(6) Agendas should be planned jointly ahead of arrival and schedules should be adhered to it as strictly as possible.

议程要双方提前商议,计划要尽量与之相符。

(7) The clear, specific, impersonal and feasible objectives will benefit the whole process of negotiation.

清晰、具体、公正、可行的目标将利于谈判的顺利进行。

(8) When the other party makes a commitment or sets a limit, one way of handling it would be to ignore it or not comprehend it or make a casual conversation or a joke.

当另一方做了承诺或者设定一个界限,接招的方法之一就是当成没听见或没理解或闲聊、开开玩笑。

(9) A motivating factor to cause such reactions is to cite principles and precedents for the other party to work with.

能够造成这种情况的一个积极因素就是举出对方的先例和原则来。

(10) It prevents the other party from concluding the negotiation prematurely and leaving without notice.

它防止对方过早地结束谈判而离开。

(11) It depends on the mood and style of negotiations whether negotiators should split into their respective teams or intermix either team.

谈判是按照双方各坐一面还是混合坐,由谈判的情绪和风格而定。

Tips

How to Respond to an Extreme Opening Offer

How should you respond to an extreme opening offer—which might set an anchor in favor of the other party? Keep in mind that an unrealistic opening offer is often simply a tactic employed by the other side, not an insult. The other party simply is trying to lower your expectation, and in the process establish its extreme offer as an anchor point. Negotiators are especially likely to use this tactic if they believe you may end up agreeing to split the difference between your reasonable offer and their extreme offer. Thus you should first recognize their extreme offer for what it is—and quickly dismiss it with a response such as "Outrageous!" or "Ridiculous—$11 000 is not in the ballpark!" The goal is to get them to abandon the possibility that their offer will be considered at all in the ensuing negotiations. Then quickly follow up with your own opening offer based on facts or a defensible position. For example: "The Blue Book on this vehicle is \$18 500, and that is for a car in an average condition. This one has low mileage and is in an excellent condition, so I believe \$20 500 is a fair price. Now what is your offer?" With this response, you accomplished two important objectives—first, you dismissed their extreme offer, effectively removing it as a potential anchor, and then you focused the discussion on your price by basing your offer on facts.

(Roger Fisher, William Ury, Bruce Patton. Getting to Yes[M]. 2nd ed. New York: Penguin Books, 1991:138-140.)

Negotiation Examples

1

A: Would you like to have a look at our exhibition center[1], Mr. Black?

B: Yes, that would be a good idea.

A: This way please.

B: Thank you.

A: Where shall we start?

B: It would take hours if I really look at everything.

A: You may be interested only in some of the items. Let's look at those.

B: Good idea. I can just have a glance at the rest.

A: Have you been in the shoes business for a long time?

B: Yes, I ve been in shoes for more than 20 years, but the company has been in business since 1951.

A: No wonder you're so experienced.

B: The shoes business has become more difficult since the competition grew[2].

A: That's true.

B: Do you have a catalog or something that tells me about your company?

A: Sure. I'll give you some later.

B: Thanks. When can we discuss some details[3]?

A: When would it be convenient for you?

B: The day after tomorrow will be fine.

Notes

(1) Would you like to have a look at our exhibition center?

请问您是否愿意来看我们的展示中心?

(2) The shoes business has become more difficult since the competition grew.

自从竞争激烈了,鞋业就不好干了。

(3) When can we discuss some details?

我们何时谈细节?

2

A: Excuse me. Are you Mr. Zhao from China?

B: Yes. And you are...

A: I'm Mr. Stevenson from New York International Company.

B: Glad to meet you. It is very nice of you to pick me up.

A: Welcome to New York.

B: Do you know where the baggage claim area is[1]?

A: Yes. It's over there. How many pieces of luggage do you have?

B: Only two suitcases.

A: Let's go to pick up your luggage.

B: OK. Here we go.

A: How was your flight?

B: Fabulous. The service is good.

A: Is this your first time to visit New York?

B: Yes. I had watched some videos on New York before I came. It's very big and crowded. The modern city has its special flavor and charm.

A: How is the business these days?

B: Not bad. I hope to expand my market and that's why I am here to negotiate with your company. Actually, I have prepared some questions like what issues your company might consider non-negotiable[2]. What topics does your company want to avoid? I even list the range of needs from optimal to minimal[3]. And now I realize that the first thing I need to know is some hobbies of your manager.

A: Well, since you think it is good for cooperation, I will tell you some favorite things my boss loves to do so that you could have a smooth negotiation, which would surely benefit both of us[4].

Notes

(1) Do you know where the baggage claim area is?

请问您知道行李提取处在哪儿吗?

(2) I had prepared some questions like what issues your company might consider non-negotiable.

我已经准备了一些问题,比如哪些问题是贵公司认为不可谈判的。

(3) I even list the range of needs from optimal to minimal.

我甚至把最大到最小的需求列了出来。

(4) I will tell you some favorite things my boss loves to do so that you could have a smooth negotiation, which would surely benefit both of us.

我想告诉你我老板最想做的几件事,这样会利于谈判的顺利进行,也使我们双方受益。

Word Bank

place a trial order 试订货
bend the rule 破例做出让步
a catalog 产品目录
a price list 价目表
quotation sheets 报价单
a sample 样品
illustrated photo prints 图片
the specifications 规格
time of shipment 装船期
terms of payment 付款方式
quick seller/quick-selling product 畅销品
conclude business with sb 成交
close a deal/close a transaction 成交

Useful Sentences

(1) But wouldn't you like to spend an extra day or two in Beijing?

你们不想在北京多待一两天吗?

(2) We've arranged our schedule without any trouble.

我们已经很顺利地把活动日程安排好了。

(3) Here is a copy of the itinerary we have worked out for you and your friends. Would you please have a look at it?

这是我们为你和你的朋友拟定的活动日程安排。请过目一下,好吗?

(4) If you have any questions on the details, feel free to ask.

如果对细节有任何疑问的话,请提出来。

(5) I can see you have put a lot of time into it.

我相信你在制订这个计划上一定花了不少精力吧。

(6) We really wish you would have a pleasant stay here.

我们真诚地希望你们在这里过得愉快。

(7) I wonder if it is possible to arrange shopping for us.

我想能否在我们访问结束时为我们安排一点时间购物。

(8) I've been looking forward to visiting your factory.

我一直都盼望着参观贵厂。

(9) Maybe we could start with the Designing Department.

也许我们可以先参观一下设计部门。

(10) Then we could look at the production line.

然后我们再去看看生产线。

(11) These drawings on the wall are process sheets.

墙上的图表是工艺流程表。

(12) So our evenings will be quite full then?

那么我们的活动在晚上也安排满了吗?

(13) We'll leave some evenings free, that is, if it is all right with you.

如果你们愿意的话,我们想留几个晚上供你们自由支配。

(14) We'd have to compare notes on what we've discussed during the day.

我们想用点时间来研究讨论一下白天谈判的情况。

(15) Is there any way of ensuring we have enough time for our talks?

我们是否能保证有充足的时间来谈判?

Tactics for Success

Use Active Listening in Bargaining

Active listening is the most useful integrative bargaining skill because it indicates that you are genuinely interested in understanding what the other person is thinking, feeling and needing. There are five tips.

(1) Maintain eye contact with the other person.

(2) Think only about what the person is saying. Resist the urge to begin formulating your reply or your position on the issue.

(3) Take notes that summarize their thoughts and can be used later as you reflect on their concerns. This attention to detail also shows your sincere interest in what they are saying.

(4) Pay close attention to their body language, including any significant aspects in your notes.

(5) Ask reflective questions to let the person know you are listening and that you understand their position. Repeat in your own words what you've heard to ensure that you have understood it and to let the other party know you understood it correctly. Ask probing questions about any aspect that is not entirely clear to you.

(Micheal Wheeler Harvard Business Essentials: Negotiation [M]. Boston: Harvard Business School Press, 2003:59.)

Exercises

Ⅰ. Translate the following words and phrases

offer without engagement

to cancel an offer

trade discount

auction price

price fluctuation

net price

floor price

50% off

total price

bid

参考价

零售价

合理的价格

销售说明书

销售额

买一送一

实盘

七五折

有竞争性的价格

老主顾

Ⅱ. Translate the following sentences

(1) We'd like to know what you can offer in this line as your sales terms, such as mode of payment, delivery, discount, etc..

(2) All your prices are on a CIF basis. We'd rather you quoted us FOB prices.

(3) Do you take special orders? That is, do you make machines according to specifications?

(4) 一般来说,收到有关信用证6个月内交货。

(5) 我们的价格比欧洲和其他各地厂商的价格都要优惠。

Do You Know

Strategy and Tactics of Distributive Bargaining

Distributive Bargaining is also called competitive or win-lose bargaining. In a distributive bargaining situation, the goals of one party are usually in fundamental and direct conflict with the goals of the other party. Resources are fixed and limited, and both parties want to maximize their share. Distributive bargaining is basically a competition over who is going to get the most of a limited resource, which is often money.

(1) **To push for a settlement close to the seller's (unknown) resistance point, thereby yielding the largest part of the settlement range for the buyer.** The buyer may attempt to influence the seller's view of what settlements are possible by making extreme offers and small concessions.

(2) **To convince the seller to change her resistance point by influencing the seller's beliefs about the value of the condo** (e. g., by telling her that the condo is overpriced), and thereby increase the bargaining range.

(3) **If a negative settlement range exists, to convince the seller to reduce her resistance point to create a positive settlement range or to change his own resistance point to create an overlap.**

（4）**To convince the seller to believe that this settlement is the best that is possible—** not that it is all she can get, or that she is incapable of getting more, or that the buyer is winning by getting more.

（Roy J Lewicki, Bruce Barry, David M Saunders. 谈判学精要[M]. 大连：东北财经大学出版社, 2008.）

Chapter 4 Negotiations on Price (Ⅰ) Inquiries

第4章 价格的谈判：询价

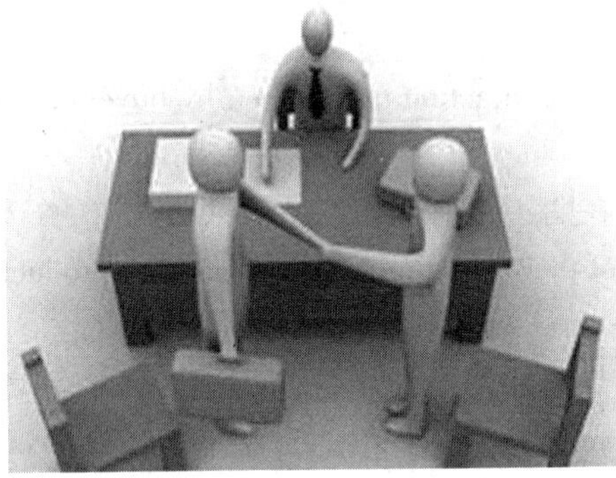

Lead-in

In the international trade practice, the terms of price influence the entire negotiation process. Price is the amount of money that is needed to acquire some combination of a product and its accompanying services. An enquiry/inquiry is a request for business information, such as price lists, catalogs, samples, and details about the goods or trade terms. It can be made by either the importer or the exporter.

Learning Objectives

In this chapter, you will be able to:

- Know how to make inquiries.
- Know how to bargain the price.

Usually, an inquiry is an action undertaken by buyers to get the products' information before purchasing[1]. It is not only one of the most direct ways to acquire product details, but also a starting point of the formal contacts between buyers and sellers[2]. In an inquiry, buyers should clearly express what kind of information is needed and under what conditions the deal can be made, and it should be brief, specific, courteous and reasonable[3]. In return, the answers to inquiries should be prompt, definite and helpful[4]. Each inquiry is a sales opportunity, an opportunity to foster a potential long-term relationship[5].

An inquiry received from abroad must be answered fully and promptly[6]. If there is no stock available for the time being, the seller should acknowledge the inquiry at once, explaining the situation and assuring that the seller would revert to it once supplies become available[7].

Notes

(1) Usually, an inquiry is an action undertaken by buyers to get the products' information before purchasing.

通常询盘是买方希望在购买之前获得产品信息而采取的行动。

(2) It is not only one of the most direct ways to acquire product details, but also a starting point of the formal contacts between buyers and sellers.

它不仅是获得产品细节的最直接的方式,而且也是买方和卖方之间合作的开始。

(3) In an inquiry, buyers should clearly express what kind of information is needed and under what conditions the deal can be made, and it should be brief, specific, courteous and reasonable.

在询价中,买方应该明确表述需要哪种信息,在什么情况下可以成交,要简单、具体、有礼、合理。

(4) In return, the answers to inquiries should be prompt, definite and helpful.

反过来,对于询价的回复要快速、确切、有助于对方了解情况。

(5) Each inquiry is a sales opportunity, an opportunity to foster a potential long-term relationship.

每一份询盘都是一次销售机会,这个机会可能会发展成一种长期的关系。

(6) An inquiry received from abroad must be answered fully and promptly.

来自国外的询盘必须要完整而快速地回复。

(7) If there is no stock available for the time being, the seller should acknowledge the inquiry at once, explaining the situation and assuring that the seller would revert to it once supplies become available.

如果暂时没有库存,卖方要立即告知对方已经收到询盘,并解释清楚没有库存的情况,要让对方了解一旦有货会马上告知。

Traps to Avoid

How to Respond to a Loaded Question

When the other party asks you a loaded question such as "Are you saying these unfair payment terms are the only ones you will accept?", how should you respond? First, prepare yourself—similar questions are often asked in negotiations. Second, don't respond emotionally with anger or by issuing your own loaded question ("Are you only willing to discuss that ridiculous opening offer you made?"). Such a response only escalates the emotions of those involved and seldom achieves anything of value to either party. Instead, be prepared to respond to a loaded question with one of these more effective alternatives.

Silence—Don't respond at all to the question, but instead return to the prior issue being discussed: "Well, let's get back to discussing..."

Humor—"Of course these terms are not the only ones I'll accept! As I tell my kids, I'm sure I have other demands you'll like even less than these!"

Take a break—"I think we all need to go outside for some fresh air."

Call it what it is—"I consider that to be a loaded question. Now if you are asking me whether these are the only payment terms I'll accept, the answer is: They are terms I put on the table, in good faith, for you to consider."

(Michael R Carrell, Christina Heavrin. Negotiating Essentials: Theory, Skills and Practices[M]. Upper Saddle River: Prentice Hall, 2010:96.)

Negotiation Examples

1

A: I'm glad to have the chance of visiting your company. I hope we can do business together.

B: It's a great honor to meet you, Mr Gao. I am sure you have seen our exhibits in the show room[1]. What in particular interests you[2]?

A: I'm interested in your hardware[3]. I've seen the exhibits and studied your catalogues[4]. Some of the items will find a ready market in America[5]. Here's a list of requirements. I'd like to have your lowest quotations, C. I. F. New York[6].

B: Thank you for your inquiry. Would you tell us what quantity you require so that we can work out the offers?[7]

A: I'll do that. At the same time, could you give me an indication of the price?[8]

B: Here are our F. O. B. prices[9]. All the prices in the lists are subject to our confirmation[10].

A: What about the commission? From European suppliers I usually get a 3 to 5 percent commission for my imports[11]. It's the general practice[12].

B: As a rule we do not allow any commission. But if the order is a sizable one, we'll consider it[13].

A：You see，I do business on a commission basis. A commission on your prices would make it easier for me to promote sales. Even 2 or 3 percent would help.

B：We'll discuss this when you place your order with us.

Notes

(1) I am sure you have seen our exhibits in the show room.

相信你已经在样品间参观了展品。

(2) What in particular interests you?

你对哪些产品特别感兴趣？

(3) I'm interested in your hardware.

我对你们的小五金有兴趣。

(4) I've seen the exhibits and studied your catalogues.

我已经看了你们的展品和商品目录。

(5) Some of the items will find a ready market in America.

我觉得有些商品在美国会很有销路。

(6) Here's a list of requirements. I'd like to have your lowest quotations，C. I. F. New York .

这是询价单，希望你们报成本加运费保险费到纽约的最低价。

(7) Would you tell us what quantity you require so that we can work out the offers?

为了便于我方提出报价，能否请你谈谈你方所需的数量？

(8) Could you give me an indication of the price?

请你们提出一个估计价格好吗？

(9) Here are our F. O. B. prices.

这是我们的装运港船上交货价的价格单。

(10) All the prices in the lists are subject to our confirmation.

单上的所有价格以我方的最后确认为准。

(11) What about the commission? From European suppliers I usually get a 3 to 5 percent commission for my imports.

那么佣金呢？我通常从欧洲的供应商那里得到3%～5%的佣金。

(12) It's the general practice.

这是一个惯例。

(13) If the order is a sizable one，we'll consider it.

如果订货数量大，我们可以考虑。

2

A: Good morning. Mr Clive. Did you have a good night sleep after the long flight from San Francisco[1]?

B: Yes, I slept well all the night.

A: OK, Mr Clive. I'm a busy man and I know you're also very busy. So let's get right to the point[2].

B: What about our inquiry? As I have mentioned, the inquiry comes from one of our clients. I hope you've brought me a firm offer.[3]

A: In fact, I came here for this matter. We value your inquiry very much, so I think it's better we go into some details before we make the firm offer[4]. You've got our catalogue and price lists?[5]

B: Yes, you gave them to me yesterday and I studied carefully in the evening.

A: The price we are going to offer is CIF Los Angeles.[6]

B: That's OK.

A: The special commission we intend to grant is 5 percent of the order over a hundred thousand US dollars in value.[7] All right?

B: CIFC 5%? It's too little. You see, it can hardly cover our expenses.[8] How about 9%?

A: I'm afraid we can't agree to 9%. You know, the distribution charges, costs and the price of raw materials are going up.[9] In fact, we've been left a small margin of profit.[10]

B: We're your old partner and bring you many orders every year.[11] We hope you'll give a special consideration.[12]

A: In that case, let's meet half way.[13] We suggest a 7% special commission for an order of US $100 000 and over in value.[14] And it will be paid in three months after the date of invoice.[15]

B: Hold on. I'll write it down. 7% special commission for an order of US $100 000 and over in value and the usual payment will be made in three months after the date of invoice. I agree. What about delivery then?

A: Your client will have to open the relevant letter of credit within 20 days after the signature of a contract and delivery can be assured within three months upon receipt of the letter of credit.[16]

B: Yes, a L/C must be opened within 20 days after the contract is signed and shipment will be made within three months upon receipt of the L/C.

A: OK?

B：It's a deal. I'll call home office as soon as possible and ask them to fax or E-mail their reply.

A：That's settled. I'll go and work out the offer.[17]

Notes

(1) Did you have a good night sleep after the long flight from San Francisco?

从洛杉矶长途飞行来此，一路辛苦，昨天夜里睡得好吧？

(2) So let's get right to the point.

让我们直奔主题吧。

(3) I hope you've brought me a firm offer.

我希望你们给我带来一个实盘。

(4) We value your inquiry very much, so I think it's better we go into some details before we make the firm offer.

我们非常重视你们的询价，所以我们最好详细深入地谈一谈，再给你们报个实盘。

(5) You've got our catalogue and price lists?

你拿到了我们的商品目录和价格单了吗？

(6) The price we are going to offer is CIF Los Angeles.

我们报的价格是 CIF 洛杉矶价。

(7) The special commission we intend to grant is 5 percent of the order over a hundred thousand US dollars in value.

凡是价值超过 10 万美元的订单，我们给予 5% 的特殊佣金。

(8) You see, it can hardly cover our expenses.

你看，这几乎都不能弥补我们的开销。

(9) You know, the distribution charges, costs and the price of raw materials are going up.

要知道，经销费用、成本价格和原材料都在上涨。

(10) In fact, we've been left a small margin of profit.

实际上，我们的余利已经不多了。

(11) We're your old partner and bring you many orders every year.

我们是你们的老顾客，每年都为你们招揽来很多订单。

(12) We hope you'll give a special consideration.

希望你们给予特殊考虑。

(13) In that case, let's meet half way.

如果那样的话，咱们各让一半。

(14) We suggest a 7% special commission for an order of US $100 000 and over in value.

对价格超过10万美元的订单,我们将给予你们7%的特殊佣金。

(15) And it will be paid in three months after the date of invoice.

在我们开出发票后三个月内付款。

(16) Your client will have to open the relevant letter of credit within 20 days after the signature of a contract and delivery can be assured within three months upon receipt of the letter of credit.

签订合同后,你们的客户必须在20天内开出信用证,我们保证在收到信用证后三个月内交货。

(17) That's settled. I'll go and work out the offer.

就这样定了,我得走了,去准备报价单。

Word Bank

inquiry/enquiry 询盘
inquirer 询价方
a general inquiry 普通询盘
import licensee 进口许可证
deliver goods from stock 现货供应
obtain a sample 收集样本
to sell at reduced rates/to sell at a discount 减价出售
a substantial drop in price 大幅度降价
fair 交易会
stamp duty 印花税
port dues 港口税
return commission 回佣
commodity 商品
representative 代表
purchase department 采购部
expand one's turnover with sb 同……扩大贸易量(营业额)
regular purchase 定期购买
special price discount 特别折扣
the enclosed detailed offer 随函报价细节
returns on investment 投资回报

net profit 净利润
current price prevailing price 现行价格(时价)
world (international) market price 国际市场价格

Useful Sentences

(1) We are enclosing herewith an inquiry sheet.
我们会随函寄出询价单一份。

(2) We are looking forward to receiving your inquiry at an early date.
盼望着早日收到你方的询价。

(3) If your prices are good, I can place the order with you right away.
如果你方价格合理,我可以马上订货。

(4) If you are interested in our electronic products, please let us know with a specific inquiry.
如果你方对我方的电子产品感兴趣,请告诉我们你方的具体询价。

(5) Your price is not reasonable. There is no chance of doing business if you don't make changes of your price.
你方价格不合理。如果不适当调整一下价格,成交的可能性不大。

(6) To produce refrigerators to your specifications will mean an alteration in our production and an increase in labor and material costs.
按照你方的价格生产冰箱需要改动生产程序,增加人力和原材料。

(7) If you could consider the quality of our product, you'll see our price is highly competitive.
如果你能从产品的质量方面去考虑的话,我方的价格是极具竞争性的。

(8) We have increased our price by a large margin.
我方确实大幅度调高了价格。

(9) For how long does your price remain open?
你方价格的有效期多长时间?

(10) We would like to ask for 10 percent off your price if we place an order over 500 000 yards.
如果我们订购50万码以上的布料,能降价10%吗?

(11) Could you tell us the quantity you require so that we can work out the offer?
为了便于我方提出报价,能否谈谈你方所需的数量?

(12) We do business on a commission basis.
我们是通过取得佣金来做生意的。

(13) Please quote the price including insurance and freight to London.

请报一个包含保险费和到伦敦的运费的报价。

(14) I must point out that some of the quotations we have received from other sources are lower than yours.

我必须告诉你们,我们从别处获得的报价比你们的要低。

(15) Please make us an offer for 5 tons of rice.

请给我们一个 5 吨大米的报价。

Tactics for Success

Attributes of Bargaining Styles

Conflict style	Strong predisposition	As a positive attribute	As a negative attribute	Weak predisposition	As a strategy
avoiding	Defers confrontational negotiation	Displays tact and diplomacy	Causes stalemates	Prefers hard-nosed bargaining	Used when not interested in negotiating
accommodating	Derives satisfaction from solving problems	Is good team-builder	May make unwise concessions	Has little patience for other party's needs	Used when hostilities need to be lessened
competing	Views negotiation as a game or sport to win	Has excellent instincts for claiming value	Focuses on issues that are easy to define as win-loss	Believes in treating people fairly and avoiding needless conflict	Used when substantive interests are important, but not the relationship
collaborating	Enjoys participating in joint problem solving	Instinctively tries to discover and satisfy the real interests of the parties	May transform a simple problem into a complex one	No patience for the give-and-take that comes with collaborative thinking	Used when relationship and the substantive outcomes are important
Compromising	Is eager to conclude negotiation on fair standards	Is best when stakes are small and time is short	Can rush the process and agree to unnecessary concessions	Refuses to compromise on principle	Used when stakes are small, time is short, or in a weak bargaining position

(Michael R Carrell, Christina Heavrin. Negotiating Essentials: Theory, Skills and Practices[M]. Upper Saddle River: Prentice Hall, 2010:12.)

Exercises

Ⅰ. Translate the following words and phrases

customs duty
landing charges
net price
price including commission
port of shipment
discount, allowance
wholesale price
retail price
export license
more or less clause
季节性折扣
具体询盘
从事外贸业务
商业关系
通信
价格术语
运费
单价
总值
金额

Ⅱ. Translate the following sentences

(1) We always allow a quantity discount if your order is large enough.

(2) The best I can offer is 800 sets with a slight increase in price, 5 dollars more than the original price.

(3) Since this is your trial order, we'll allow you a commission of 2% as an encouragement for future business.

(4) 按照公司的惯例,是不给任何佣金的。

(5) 按这个数量订货,我可以给你10%的优惠。

Do You Know

Management of Tangibles

Successful negotiation involves the management of tangibles (e. g. , the price or the terms of agreement) and also the resolution of intangibles. Intangible factors are the underlying psychological motivations that may directly or indirectly influence the parties during a negotiation. Some examples of intangibles are ① the need to "win", beat the other party, or avoid losing to the other party; ② the need to look "good", "competent", or "tough" to the people you represent; ③ the need to defend an important principle or precedent in a negotiation; and ④ the need to appear "fair", or "honorable" or to protect one's reputation.

(Roy J Lewicki, Bruce Barry, David M Saunders. 谈判学精要[M]. 大连: 东北财经大学出版社, 2008.)

Chapter 5　Negotiations on Price (Ⅱ) Offers and Counter-offers

第 5 章　价格的谈判：报盘和还盘

Lead-in

An offer refers to the process that the buyer or the seller gives some sales terms and conditions to the other party for confirmation and intends to sign a legal and effective contract based on these terms and conditions. If the offer cannot meet all the satisfaction of the offeree, he may amend and add some new terms and requirements. It is called counter-offer.

Learning Objectives

In this chapter, you will be able to:

- Learn how to make offers and counter-offers.
- Know how to bargain the price.

An offer refers to the process that the buyer or the seller gives some sales terms and conditions to the other party for confirmation and intends to sign a legal and effective contract based on these terms and conditions[1]. Usually, an offer will be provided by either the seller with a sales offer or the buyer with a purchase offer. Offers include firm offer[2] and non-firm offer[3]. A firm offer refers to a promise of selling or buying the goods at a certain time according to the agreed price. Once the other party accepts the offer, it should not be cancelled or changed. On the contrary, a non-firm offer is just an expression of accepting the transaction terms without any legal promise.

An offer contains not only the price but also all the trade terms such as quantity, quality, payment terms, delivery date, time of shipment, package, validity and so on[4].

The differences between a firm offer and a non-firm offer are as follows.

(1) It is unnecessary to cover all the trade terms in the non-firm offer.

(2) Reservations such as "subject to our final confirmation", "subject to goods being unsold", "without engagement" symbolize the non-firm offer.

(3) Words such as "about", or "reference price" should not be used in the firm offer to avoid the ambiguity.

By being fully involved in the market, the buyer can pick up a large amount of information, which is accomplished through frequent visits to various types of resources, conversations with salespeople, reading newspapers and trade journals, watching competitors' advertising and offerings, and studying the catalogs and price lists of vendors.[5]

There are various international trade terms and the following are the most frequently used.

(1) The following can be used only for sea or inland waterway transport.[6]

FOB—FREE on BOARD (named port of shipment): the seller delivers when the goods pass the ship's rail at the named port of shipment. The buyer has to bear all costs and risks of loss of or damage to the goods from that point. The seller needs to clear the goods for export.[7]

CFR—COST and FREIGHT (named port of destination): the seller delivers when the goods pass the ship's rail at the port of shipment. The seller must pay the costs and freight necessary to bring the goods to the named port of destination. The risk of loss of or damage to the goods, as well as any additional costs due to any events occurring after the time of delivery, is transferred from the seller to the buyer. The seller needs to clear the goods for export.[8]

CIF—COST, INSURANCE and FREIGHT (named port of destination): the seller delivers when the goods pass the ship's rail at the port of shipment. The seller must pay the costs and freight necessary to bring the goods to the named port of destination. The risk of loss of or damage to the goods, as well as any additional costs due to any events occurring after the time of delivery, is transferred from the seller to the buyer. However, in CIF the seller also has to procure marine insurance against the buyer's risk of loss of or damage to the carriage. Consequently, the seller contracts for insurance and pays the insurance premium.[9]

(2) The following can be used irrespective of the mode of transport including multimodal transport.

FCA—FREE CARRIER(named place): the seller delivers the goods, cleared for export, to the carrier nominated by the buyer in the named place. If delivery occurs at the seller's premises, the seller is responsible for loading. If delivery occurs in any other place, the seller is not responsible for unloading. [10]

CPT—CARRIAGE PAID to(named place of destination): the seller delivers the goods to the carrier nominated by himself, but the seller must in addition pay the cost of carriage necessary to bring the goods to the named destination. The buyer bears all risks and any other costs occurring after the goods have been so delivered. [11]

CIP—CARRIAGE and INSURANCE PAID to (named place of destination): the seller delivers the goods to the carrier nominated by himself, but the seller must in addition pay the cost of carriage necessary to bring the goods to the named destination. The buyer bears all risks and any additional costs occurring after the goods have been so delivered. However, in CIP the seller also has to procure marine insurance against the buyer's risk of loss of or damage to the carriage. Consequently, the seller contracts for insurance and pays the insurance premium. [12]

Notes

(1) An offer refers to the process that the buyer or the seller gives some sales terms and conditions to the other party for confirmation and intends to sign a legal and effective contract based on these terms and conditions.

发盘指的是交易一方向对方提出待确认的主要交易条款与条件。若对方予以接收，即可签署具有法律效力的交易合同。

(2) firm offer: 实盘

(3) non-firm offer: 虚盘

(4) An offer contains not only the price but also all the trade terms such as quantity, quality, payment terms, delivery date, time of shipment, package, validity and so on.

报盘需包括所有交易条款，如价格、数量、质量、支付条件、交货日期、装运期限、包装、有效期等。

(5) By being fully involved in the market, the buyer can pick up a considerable information, which is accomplished through frequent visits to various types of resources, conversations with salespeople, reading newspapers and trade journals, watching competitors' advertising and offerings, and studying the catalogs and price lists of vendors.

通过频繁探查各类资源、与销售人员对话、浏览报纸和贸易报刊、查看竞争者广告及其报盘、研究供应商产品目录及价目表等方式广泛接触市场,买方可以获取大量宝贵信息。

(6) The following can be used only for sea or inland waterway transport.

下列术语仅适用于海运或内河运输。

(7) FOB—FREE on BOARD (named port of shipment): the seller delivers when the goods pass the ship's rail at the named part of shipment. The buyer has to bear all costs and risks of loss of or damage to the goods from that point. The seller needs to clear the goods for export.

船上交货(指定装运港):当货物在指定的装运港越过船舷,卖方即完成交货。买方必须从该点起承担货物灭失或损坏的一切风险。卖方办理货物出口清关手续。

(8) CFR—COST and FREIGHT (named port of destination): the seller delivers when the goods pass the ship's rail at the port of shipment. The seller must pay the costs and freight necessary to bring the goods to the named port of destination. The risk of loss of or damage to the goods, as well as any additional costs due to any events occurring after the time of delivery, is transferred from the seller to the buyer. The seller needs to clear the goods for export.

成本加运费(指定目的港):在装运港货物越过船舷卖方即完成交货,卖方必须支付将货物运至指定的目的港所需的运费和费用。但交货后货物灭失或损坏的风险,以及由于各种事件造成的任何额外费用,即由卖方转移到买方。卖方办理货物出口清关手续。

(9) CIF—COST, INSURANCE and FREIGHT (named port of destination): the seller delivers when the goods pass the ship's rail at the port of shipment. The seller must pay the costs and freight necessary to bring the goods to the named port of destination. The risk of loss of or damage to the goods, as well as any additional costs due to any events occurring after the time of delivery, is transferred from the seller to the buyer. However, in CIF the seller also has to procure marine insurance against the buyer's risk of loss of or damage to the carriage. Consequently, the seller contracts for insurance and pays the insurance premium.

成本、保险费加运费(指定目的港):在装运港货物越过船舷卖方即完成交货,卖方必须支付将货物运至指定的目的港所需的运费和费用。但交货后货物灭失或损坏的风险,以及由于各种事件造成的任何额外费用,即由卖方转移到买方。但是在 CIF 条件下,卖方还必须办理买方货物在运输途中灭失或损坏风险的海运保险。因此,由卖方订立保险合同并支付保险费。

(10) FCA—FREE CARRIER(named place): the seller delivers the goods, cleared for export, to the carrier nominated by the buyer in the named place. If delivery occurs at the seller's premises, the seller is responsible for loading. If delivery occurs in any other place, the

seller is not responsible for unloading.

货交承运人(指定地点)：卖方只要将货物在指定的地点交给买方指定的承运人,并办理了出口清关手续,即完成交货。若卖方在其所在地交货,则卖方应负责装货,若卖方在任何其他地点交货,卖方则不负责卸货。

(11) CPT—CARRIAGE PAID to (named place of destination): the seller delivers the goods to the carrier nominated by himself, but the seller must in addition pay the cost of carriage necessary to bring the goods to the named destination. The buyer bears all risks and any other costs occurring after the goods have been so delivered.

运费付至(指定地点)：卖方向其指定的承运人交货,但卖方还必须支付将货物运至目的地的运费。亦即买方承担交货之后一切风险和其他费用。

(12) CIP—CARRIAGE and INSURANCE PAID to (named place of destination): the seller delivers the goods to the carrier nominated by himself, but the seller must in addition pay the cost of carriage necessary to bring the goods to the named destination. The buyer bears all risks and any additional costs occurring after the goods have been so delivered. However, in CIP the seller also has to procure marine insurance against the buyer's risk of loss of or damage to the carriage. Consequently, the seller contracts for insurance and pays the insurance premium.

运费和保险费付至(指定目的地)：卖方向其指定的承运人交货,但卖方还必须支付将货物运至目的地的运费。亦即买方承担交货之后一切风险和其他费用。但是在 CIP 条件下,卖方必须办理买方货物在运输途中灭失或损坏风险的海运保险。因此,由卖方订立保险合同并支付保险费。

Case Study

Lowball Offer

A corporate executive moving to a new city looked at about 20 pieces of property one weekend with his real estate agent. One was a large condo within a block of his new office, with a great view of a river. The asking price was $300 000. Unfortunately, however, the previous tenants were the teenage sons of a wealthy business man who had moved out six months before his sons—who then completely trashed the condo. The prospective buyer's agent called him late one night to let him know the condo owner's agent had confided in her that the owner wanted to sell it quickly. "I would need to spend $100 000 just to have it gutted and refurbished." The executive replied to her suggestion that he made an offer. "Fine, then offer them half." She said. Thinking he had no chance of getting it at $150 000, the owner, 6000 miles away and wanting to unload the condo, accepted the lowball offer. It worked because this situation involved unusual circumstances that caused the market price to be less relevant.

Negotiation Examples

1

A: Hello, Angela. I'm pleased that you are still here. I am making you the offer for mobile phones[1].

B: Thank you for responding to my inquiry so quickly.[2]

A: Sure. You're a big buyer[3]. Our offer is for 500 mobile phones, US $3200 each CFR Los Angeles.[4]

B: I have to say this price is beyond my expectation.[5] You know, Mr. Song, your mobile phones are not as well known as international big brands.[6] It will cost us a lot to promote your products here.[7] And it is risky for us to do that. We wish you would reconsider your price.[8] Probably you could lower your price by 10%.[9]

A: Our mobile phones are very competitive against the famous brands.[10] And they are not as expensive as big brands. I can ensure the good quality of our products and people will love the fashionable style of the phones.[11]

B: I still believe 10% reduction is really reasonable for all the efforts and risk.[12]

A: I know you will try your best to increase the sales of our mobile phones. We really appreciate your efforts in promoting our products in your market.[13] When we make this offer, we have already taken every factor into consideration. How about a 5% reduction? That's all I can do.

B: OK. I will report it to my supervisor and get back to you before 15th of this month.[14]

Notes

(1) I am making you the offer for mobile phones.
这是手机的报盘。

(2) Thank you for responding to my inquiry so quickly.
谢谢您这么快就答复我的询盘。

(3) You're a big buyer.
你们可是大买主。

(4) Our offer is for 500 mobile phones, US $3200 each CFR Los Angeles.
我们的500部手机,洛杉矶成本加运费价格每部3200美元。

(5) I have to say this price is beyond my expectation.

这可不是我预期的价格。

(6) Your mobile phones are not as well known as international big brands.

你们的手机不像那些国际名牌广为人知。

(7) It will cost us a lot to promote your products here. And it is risky for us to do that.

推销你们的产品将花费我们大量的资金。我们这么做的风险也很大。

(8) We wish you would reconsider your price.

我们希望你们能够重新考虑价格。

(9) Probably you could lower your price by 10%.

希望你们能降价10%。

(10) Our mobile phones are very competitive against the famous brands.

我们的手机同那些名牌比也很有竞争力。

(11) I can ensure the good quality of our products and people will love the fashionable style of the phones.

我能保证我们产品的质量,人们会喜欢我们手机的流行款式。

(12) I still believe 10% reduction is really reasonable for all the efforts and risk.

以所付出的努力和承担的风险来看,10%让利是相当合理的。

(13) We really appreciate your efforts in promoting our products in your market.

若你方帮助我们将产品打入你方市场,我们将不胜感激。

(14) I will report it to my supervisor and get back to you before 15th of this month.

我会同我们负责人商量。本月15日前给您答复。

2

A: This is our rock-bottom price[1], Mr. Zhou. We can't make any further concessions.[2]

B: If that's the case, there's not much point in further discussion. We might as well call the whole deal off.[3]

A: We'll never be able to come down to your price. The gap is too big.[4]

B: I think it unwise for both of us to insist on the original price.[5] How about meeting each other half way and each makes a further concession so that the business can be concluded?[6]

A: What is your proposal?

B: Your unit price is 80 dollars higher than we can accept. May I suggest we meet each other half way, I meant it literally.[7]

A: Do you mean to suggest that we have to make a further reduction of 40 dollars in our price? That's impossible.

B: What would you suggest?

A: The best we can do will be a reduction of another 20 dollars. That'll definitely be the rock-bottom.

B: That still leaves a gap of 60 dollars to be covered.[8] Let's meet each other half way once more, then the gap will be closed and we can make it a deal.

A: All right. Actually, I intend to have a long relationship with your company. My friends in the business circles all seem to agree that Chinese import and export corporations have become more flexible in doing business recently.[9]

B: Yes, they're right. Actually, we have restored or adopted international practices in our foreign trade.[10]

A: I'm very pleased to hear that. In order to expand the bilateral relations between our two parties, and in particular, exchanging timely views on specific problems in the execution and enforcement of contracts,[11] is it possible for us to have a representative that could stay permanently in Shanghai?

B: Basically speaking, yes. We welcome the establishment of representative offices by foreign companies in Shanghai. Of course, there are more details to be talked over. We can negotiate next time.

Notes

(1) This is our rock-bottom price.

这是我方的最低价格。

(2) We can't make any further concessions.

我方不可能再让了。

(3) We might as well call the whole deal off.

我们是不是干脆放弃这笔生意算了。

(4) We'll never be able to come down to your price. The gap is too big.

我们的价格绝对不可能降到你方提出的水平,差距太大了。

(5) I think it unwise for both of us to insist on the original price.

如果我们双方都坚持自己的价格是不明智的。

(6) How about meeting each other half way and each makes a further concession so that the business can be concluded?

各方都再让一半,生意就能成交了。

(7) Your unit price is 80 dollars higher than we can accept. May I suggest we meet each

other half way, I meant it literally.

你方提出的单价比我们可以接受的价格高出80美元,我说的各让一半,是名副其实的一半。

(8) That still leaves a gap of 60 dollars to be covered.

这样还剩下60美元的差额呀。

(9) My friends in the business circles all seem to agree that Chinese import and export corporations have become more flexible in doing business recently.

我商业界的许多朋友好像觉得中国的进出口公司在贸易中做法更加灵活了。

(10) Actually, we have restored or adopted international practices in our foreign trade.

事实上,最近我们在国际贸易中恢复和采用了国际管理的习惯做法。

(11) In order to expand the bilateral relations between our two parties, and in particular, exchanging timely views on specific problems in the execution and enforcement of contracts.

为了发展我们双边的关系,特别是为了在执行合同过程中就具体问题及时交换意见。

Word Bank

to accept an offer 接受报盘

to entertain an offer 考虑报盘

to submit an offer 提交报盘

to extend an offer 延长报盘

to renew/reinstate an offer 恢复报盘

to withdraw an offer 撤回报盘

to decline/turn down an offer 谢绝报盘

price fluctuation 价格波动

counter offer 还盘

to make a concession in price/to make a price reduction/to cut down the price by/reduce the price by/bring down the price to 降价

an acceptable price/an attractive price 可接受的价格

a favorable price 优惠价

end-of-month sale (EOM Sale) 月底大降价

high, medium, low grade 上、中、下级

to make a concession in price/reduce the price by/bring down the price to 让步

to make an offer for 对……报盘(报价)

non-firm offer 虚盘

firm offer 实盘

commission 佣金
offer subject to seller's confirmation 需经卖方确认的发盘
offer subject to our written acceptance 以我方书面接受为准的报盘
offer subject to export/import license 以获得出口(进口)许可证为准的报盘
offer subject to prior sale 以提前售出为准的报盘
offer subject to goods being unsold 以商品未售出为准的报盘
offer subject to your reply reaching here 以你方答复到达我地为准的报盘
offer subject to sample approval 以样品确定后生效为准的报盘
offer subject to our final confirmation 以我方最后确认为准的报盘

Useful Sentences

(1) What's the wholesale price? What's the retail price?
批发价是多少？零售价是多少？
(2) Can you give me a price discount?
能不能给我打折？
(3) I'll give you half way, OK?
我让你一半，怎样？
(4) How much would you like it to be?
你想出什么价？
(5) Here are our latest price sheets.
这是我们最新的报价单。
(6) It is a small deal and can't go cheaper.
这个是小生意，不可以再便宜了。
(7) It is almost at cost.
这几乎是成本价。
(8) We'll reduce the price if your order is large.
假如你们的订货量大，我们可以减价。
(9) The size of our order depends on your price.
我们订的数量取决于你们的价格。
(10) There is no profit at this price.
这个价我们没利可赚。
(11) I'm sure I will sell it to you if there are profits.
如果这个价有钱赚，我一定卖给你。

(12) Can we meet each other half way?

能不能互相让步一半?

(13) The offer will remain open for 6 days.

此报价单将开放6天时间。

(14) Is your offer a firm one or the one subject to final confirmation?

你报的是实盘还是以最后确认的为准?

(15) We hope that our quotation will be a satisfactory one and expect your orders.

希望你们能满意我方的报价,期待接到你们的订单。

Tactics for Success

Guidelines for Making Concessions

(1) Give yourself enough room to make concessions.

(2) Try to get the other party to start revealing their needs and objectives first.

(3) Be the first to concede on a minor issue but not the first to concede on a major issue.

(4) Make unimportant concessions and portray them as more valuable than they are.

(5) Make the other party work hard for every concession you make.

(6) Use trade-offs to obtain something for every concession you make.

(7) Generally, concede slowly and give a little with each concession.

(8) Do not reveal your deadline to the other party.

(9) Occasionally say "no" to the other negotiator.

(10) Be careful trying to take back concessions even in "tentative" negotiations.

(11) Keep a record of concessions made in the negotiation to try to identify a pattern.

(12) Do not concede "too often, too soon, or too much."

(D W Hendon, M H Roy, Z U Ahmed. Negotiation Concession Patterns: a Multicountry, Multiperiod Study[J]. American Review, 2003(21):75-83.)

Exercises

Ⅰ. Translate the following words and phrases

rebate

to extend an offer

to renew an offer

to withdraw an offer

monopoly price
a favorable price
FOB
CIF
CFR
CIP
价格条款
合理的价格
报价
有销路
折扣
给予某人……的佣金
销售确认书
销售合同
讨价还价
可接受的价格

Ⅱ. Translate the following sentences

(1) We hope you will take advantage of this favorable offer and send us your acceptance at an early date.

(2) This is the best quotation we can make. We consider it a rock-bottom price.

(3) You will find that we have given you the most favorable quotation.

(4) 你方的报价不能接受。

(5) 抱歉,我们不得不拒绝你方报盘。

Do You Know

Example of Communication Rules for International Negotiators

Never touch a Malay on the top of the head, for that is where the soul resides. Never show the sole of your shoe to an Arab, for it is dirty and represents the bottom of the body, and never use your left hand in Muslim culture, for it is reserved for physical hygiene. Touch the side of your nose in Italy and it is a sign of distrust. Always look directly and intently into your French associate's eye when making an important point. Direct eye contact in Southeast Asia, however, should be avoided until the relationship is firmly established. If your Japanese associate has just sucked air in deeply through his teeth, that's a sign you've got real problems. Your Mexican associate will want to embrace you at the end of a long and successful negotiation; so will your Central and Eastern European associates, who may give you a bear hug and kiss you three times on alternating cheeks. Americans often stand farther apart than their Latin and Arab associates but closer than their Asian associates. In the United States people shake hands forcefully and enduringly; in Europe a handshake is usually quick and to the point; in Asia, it is often rather limp. Laughter and giggling in the West Indies indicates humor; in Asia, it more often indicates embarrassment and humility. Additionally, the public expression of deep emotion is considered ill-mannered in most countries of the Pacific Rim; there is an extreme separation between one's personal and public selves. Withholding emotion in Latin America, however, is often cause for mistrust.

(D A Foster. Bargaining across Borders: How to Negotiate Business Successfully Anywhere in the World [M]. New York: McGraw-Hill. 1992:281.)

Chapter 6 Placing an Order

第6章 订 货

Lead-in

An order refers to an oral or written request to supply a specified quantity of goods. It may be the result of an offer or a counter-offer with a positive acceptance. When the seller receives an order, he must send a confirmation of sales.

Learning Objectives

In this chapter, you will be able to:

- Learn how to place an order.
- Know strategies in placing an order.

After inquiry, quotation, rounds of offers and counter offers are made, both parties come to an agreement and the buyer places an order to the seller. [1] An order is an offer to buy, and it is a common form of correspondence for obtaining specified goods or services. [2] The order describes what the buyer wants to buy, what it will pay for the goods. [3]

Accuracy and clarity are the essential qualities of an order. An order should include:

(1) Name of commodity, item number, specifications such as size and color;

(2) Quantity or weight;

(3) Price, including unit price and amount;

(4) Package;

(5) Date and method of shipment;

(6) Terms of payment.

An order should be acknowledged immediately upon receipt.[4] If the seller accepts it, he or she had better repeat the terms and remember to deliver the good will in the closing section of the letter.[5] However, there are times when the seller partially or can not accept the buyer's orders owing to the limited stock or price fluctuation. In such circumstances, great care should be taken when writing a rejection so as to cause no harm to future business.[6]

Notes

(1) After inquiry, quotation, rounds of offers and counter offers are made, both parties come to an agreement and the buyer places an order to the seller.

在询盘、报价和往返多次的报盘和还盘后,在双方都同意的情况下,买方就会下订单。

(2) An order is an offer to buy, and it is a common form of correspondence for obtaining specified goods or services.

订单就是提出购买要求,是一种非常普通的要求获得某种商品或者服务的信件。

(3) The order describes what the buyer wants to buy, what it will pay for the goods.

订单说明买方要买什么、要付多少钱。

(4) An order should be acknowledged immediately upon receipt.

买方收到订单后须及时予以确认。

(5) If the seller accepts it, he or she had better repeat the terms and remember to deliver the good will in the closing section of the letter.

如果接受订单,最好在回复时重申订单条款,并在结尾时表达良好祝愿。

(6) However, there are times when the seller partially or cannot accept the buyer's orders owing to the limited stock or price fluctuation. In such circumstances, great care should be taken when writing a rejection so as to cause no harm to future business.

但是有时卖方由于库存有限或价格波动部分或者无法接受买方订单,这种情况下在写回信时应特别小心,以免以后的买卖受到影响。

Traps to Avoid

Silence Is Golden

When negotiations reach a critical point—such as when one party makes a verbal attack, refuses to make any concessions, or threatens to walk out—one tactic that might turn the tide is silence. A negotiator who says nothing in response to a verbal attack, unreasonable demand, or threat does, in fact, send a clear signal to the other party. Often, after a few minutes of silence, the negotiator who caused the breakdown will feel uncomfortable and make a conciliatory statement or concession in order to get the other party to continue to negotiate. If not, the silent party has not lost anything, and most likely will have communicated his or her displeasure with the actions of the other side. Experienced negotiators have learned that "silence is golden" when applied in appropriate situations.

(Michael R Carrell, Christina Heavrin. The Everyday Negotiator[M]. Amherst: HRD Press, 2004: 118-121.)

Negotiation Examples

1

A: We'd like to order 3000 pieces of this type of leather shoes.[1]

B: I'm terribly sorry. Leather shoes are our best selling goods. They are sold out fast every year.[2] I m afraid we can't meet your requirement.[3]

A: We are your regular customer, so please give us some priority on supply.[4]

B: Well, according to regulations, we can only supply each customer 800 pieces,[5] but I will make an exception and give you 200 pieces more.[6] That's the best I can do.

A: The day before yesterday, I sent the offer you made to my head office. It is 10% higher than that of the previous year.[7] Both of us need to move forward to make an agreement.

B: We are glad that you have the interest to do business with us. But our costs have risen greatly. The best I can do is to keep the increase down to 8%. I'm sure our leather shoes will find a ready market in your area at such a low price.[8]

A: Even 8% increase is still high. Since we cooperate for many times and our orders are big, 3000 pieces, with 400 pieces more than the previous order, how about 6%?

B: We can't do so much. If you agree, 7% is OK.

A: Well, I accept it.

B: That's really the rock bottom price we can offer. Then we make you a special offer of these leather shoes at US $30 each piece. We would deliver them in July.[9] Are you certain that the necessary L/Cs reach us 20 days before each shipment?

A: I will see to it personally.[10]

Notes

(1) We'd like to order 3000 pieces of this type of leather shoes.

我方想订购3000双这种皮鞋。

(2) They are sold out fast every year.

每年销售特快。

(3) I'm afraid we can't meet your requirement.

恐怕我们难以满足贵方要求。

(4) We are your regular customer, so please give us some priority on supply.

我们是你们的老客户,请在供货方面给我们一些优待。

(5) Well, according to regulations, we can only supply each customer 800 pieces.

好吧,按规定,我们只供给每位客户800双。

(6) But I will make an exception and give you 200 pieces more.

但我例外多给了您200双。

(7) It is 10% higher than that of the previous year.

比去年的价格高10%。

(8) I'm sure our leather shoes will find a ready market in your area at such a low price.

我相信我方的皮鞋按照这个低价肯定会在你方市场畅销。

(9) We would deliver them in July.

我们将会在7月交货。

(10) I will see to it personally.

我会亲自处理此事。

2

A: Hello, Mr. Jones, welcome to our company.

B: Hi. Nice to meet you. We have had your offer and are very much interested.

A: Do you find that our specifications meet your requirements?[1] I'm sure the prices we suggest are competitive.[2]

A: Sure. I came here to place the order with you.[3] We love the design of your laces.[4] Later, my company will send you an official confirmation.[5]

B: I see, we quoted you ex-warehouse prices.[6] Do you want me to give you the FOB prices?[7] That would cover transport from our warehouse to the docks, and all the handling and shipping charges including wharfage, dock dues, porterage, and port rates.[8] You will be responsible for the sea freight and marine insurance.[9]

A: But we prefer to the total cost delivered right to our port.[10]

B: How about a CIF price?[11] That would cover the cost of the goods to make them seaworthy; a comprehensive insurance, with the clause from warehouse to warehouse; all the forwarding and shipping charges and the freight paid to your port.[12]

A: But there will be a few things left for us to pay.

B: OK. The charges for your forwarding agent include fees for clearing the goods, paying the customs duties, and arranging the deliver to your site. I can get CIF prices worked out by our shipping department while we go on talking.[13] Ms. Liu, take these price quotations to the shipping department and get them to work out CIF prices for Mr. Jones, won't you?[14]

A: OK.

B: It is a pleasure to talk with you.

Notes

(1) Do you find that our specifications meet your requirements?
不知道您认为我们的规格是否符合你们的要求?

(2) I'm sure the prices we suggest are competitive.
我确信我们提出的价格是非常有竞争力的。

(3) I came here to place the order with you.
我此次来访正是向贵公司订货的。

(4) We love the design of your laces.
我们喜欢你们蕾丝的设计。

(5) Later, my company will send you an official confirmation.
我公司将很快邮寄给您一份正式确认书。

(6) I see, we quoted you ex-warehouse prices.
我想报的是工厂交货价。

(7) Do you want me to give you the FOB prices?
您希望我报离岸价吗?

(8) That would cover transport from our warehouse to the docks, and all the handling and shipping charges including wharfage, dock dues, porterage, and port rates.

包括从我方仓库到码头的运费、理货费和装运费，装运费包括码头费用、搬运费用、船坞使用费和入港税。

(9) You will be responsible for the sea freight and marine insurance.

由贵方支付海运费和海运保险费。

(10) But we prefer to the total cost delivered right to our port.

我们想把全部的费用考虑进去,包括直接到我们的港口。

(11) How about a CIF price?

到岸价好吗?

(12) That would cover the cost of the goods to make them seaworthy; a comprehensive insurance, with the clause from warehouse to warehouse; all the forwarding and shipping charges and the freight paid to your port.

包括适于海运货物成本; 综合保费,含有"仓至仓"条款; 所有运输和装船费用,及到贵方港口的运费。

(13) The charges for your forwarding agent include fees for clearing the goods, paying the customs duties, and arranging the deliver to your site. I can get CIF prices worked out by our shipping department while we go on talking.

如你方运输行负责办理货物报关的费用、缴纳关税以及把货物运至贵方指定地点的费用。我会让我们的货运部门计算出到岸价的。

(14) Ms. Liu, take these price quotations to the shipping department and get them to work out CIF prices for Mr. Jones, won't you?

刘小姐,请把这些报价单送到货运部,让他们为琼斯先生计算出到岸价价格。

Word Bank

place a trial order 试订货

bend the rule 破例做出让步

indent 订单

book; booking 订货;订购

cable reply 电复

limited stock 库存有限

out of stock 无现货

price indication 指示性价格

reply immediately 速复

business negotiation 交易磋商

without engagement 不受约束

valid till 有效至
breach of the agreement 订购合同
to sign a contract/to conclude a contract 履行合同
to carry out the contract 严守合同
to scrap a contract/to rescind a contract/to annul a contract 取消合同
to extend a contract/to renew a contract 延长合同
to amend a contract/to amend relevant contract terms 修改合同
carry out/execute/fill/fulfil an order 执行订单
rescind/revoke/withdraw an order 取消订单
cancel an order 取消订货
decline an order 谢绝订货
accept/book your order 接受你方订货
repeat order 重复订单
pending order 待办订单
to keep a business going under difficult circumstances 惨淡经营
business scope/business range/line of business 经营范围
business diversification 经营多样化
management and administration 经营管理
the original and copies of the contract 合同正本与副本
commercial liability 商务责任
general terms and conditions 一般交易条件
subject to prior sale 以未售出为准

Useful Sentences

(1) Could I have your latest catalogues or something that tells me about your company?
可以给我一些贵公司最近的商品价格目录表或者一些有关说明资料吗?

(2) I hope to conclude some business with you.
我希望能与贵公司建立贸易关系。

(3) We have complied with your request for a change in your order.
我们已经根据您的要求,修订了订单。

(4) As a result of the exchange of letters between us, we have now come to terms.
经过双方信函来往,我们终于达成交易。

(5) We have pleasure to enclose herewith our contract No. 6 in two originals for your counter-signature. Please send us one copy back at your earliest convenience.

现附我方第6号合同正本一式两份,请会签,并尽早寄回一份。

(6) We regret to inform you that due to our heavy commitments, we are unable to entertain any new order. But we are keeping your inquiry before us and, as soon as we are in a position to accept new orders, we will contact you by fax.

今遗憾告知您,因为我方手头订单过多,暂时无法接受商品的新订单。不过,我方将关注你方询盘,一旦能够接受新订单,将用电传与你方联系。

(7) Please notice the fact that the stipulations in the relevant credit should strictly conform to the terms stated in our S/C so as to avoid subsequent amendments.

请注意,信用证条款必须与我方销售确认书条款完全相符,以免日后修改。

(8) We regret to inform you that there is no market for the high priced goods at this end. Please offer only the goods of the medium price range.

今歉告,本地市场没有高价商品的销路,敬请提供中等价格的商品。

(9) We need the goods in time so as to take advantage of the present demand. If there is any delay in shipment, we will be compelled to cancel the order.

货物必须准时到达,以便我方利用目前市场需求。如装运延误,我方将被迫取消这次货物订单。

(10) We appreciate your cooperation and hope to receive your further orders.

谢谢你方合作,盼望收到你方更多的订单。

(11) Your order is receiving our immediate attention and you can depend on us to effect delivery well within your time limit.

你方订单正在及时处理,你可信赖我方将会在规定时间内发运。

(12) The best we can do is to make you a special offer at 20 U. S. dollars per kilogram.

我们最多给您报个特别优惠价,每千克20美元。

(13) I'm ready to place an order with you, but the only condition is that the goods are confined to Britain.

我准备向你们订货,但唯一的条件是货物只限卖给英国。

(14) Once we get your purchase order, we'll begin preparing the goods.

我们一接到您的订单就开始备货。

(15) Do you usually buy in large quantities?

你们的订购量通常都很大吗?

Tips

A Field Analysis of Negotiation

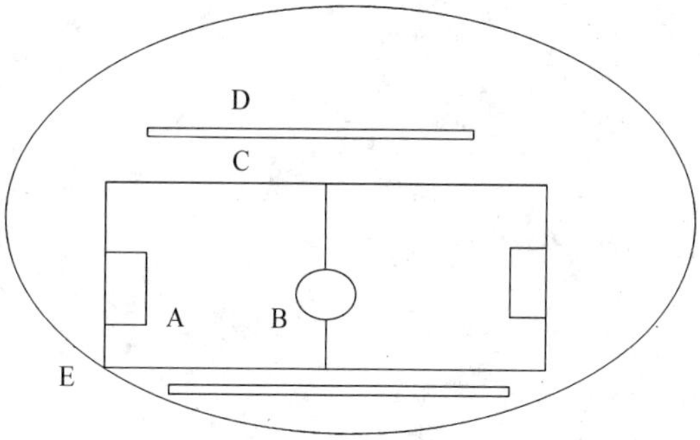

A. The direct actors (who is on the field on our side?)

B. The opposition actors (who is on the field on their side?)

C. Indirect actors (who is on the sidelines?)

D. Interested observers (who is in the stands?)

E. Environmental factors (what is going on the broad environment of the game—outside the stadium, but shaping and defining what happens in the stadium?)

(Roy J Lewicki, Bruce Barry, David M Saunders. 谈判学精要[M]. 大连：东北财经大学出版社，2008:103.)

Exercises

Ⅰ. Translate the following words and phrases

exclusive selling
commercial representative
commercial disputes
commercial cases/commercial action
commercial arbitration
management decision
scale operation
to purchase confirmation
terminate a contract

time of validity
经营战略
经营
合同条款
销售确认书
习惯做法
业务洽谈
参考价
销售合同
电子商务
购货合同

Ⅱ. Translate the following sentences

(1) As the goods you ordered are now in stock, we will ship them without fail by the leaving Shanghai on 12th April.

(2) We would grant those who can help us with prompt payment the priority, which will speed up our capital operation.

(3) We regret that we cannot book the order at the prices we quoted five weeks ago.

(4) 我们今天会寄上正式的订单。

(5) 订购的货品目前已经无存货。

Do You Know

The Connect Model and the Requirements for Building a Relationship

Four Requirements	Process Model
(1) Can we agree to have a constructive conversation?	Commit to the relationship—signal that you are ready to work on the problem and it is worth doing. Optimize safety—you will do your best to not make the other feel defensive, and you will try to appreciate the other's point of view
(2) Can our conversation be productive enough to make a difference?	Narrow the discussion to one issue—identify one issue at a time in a nonthreatening way. Neutralize defensiveness—minimize using words, terms, or descriptions that make the other defensive
(3) Can we understand and appreciate each other's perspective?	Explain and echo perspective—tell the other what you observe, how it makes you feel, and the long-term consequences

续表

Four Requirements	Process Model
(4) Can we all commit to making improvements?	Change one behavior each—agree that each of you is going to change one behavior. Track it! —determine ways to monitor progress

(F Lofasto, C Larson. When Teams Work Best[M]. Thousand Oaks: SAGE, 2001:51.)

Chapter 7 Negotiations on Payment Terms
第 7 章　付款条件的谈判

Lead-in

This chapter specifies different methods of payment (letter of credit, remittance, collection) because both exporters and importers may be faced with risks.

Learning Objectives

In this chapter, you will be able to:

- Know how to negotiate payment terms.
- Learn strategies in negotiating payment terms.

Both exporters and importers face risks in the transactions due to the other party's failure to fulfill the contract. In order to prevent such jeopardy, different methods of payment have been developed. The modes can be generally divided into three categories:

(1) Letter of credit;

(2) Remittance;

(3) Collection.

L/C belongs to banker's credit, which means it is the banker's responsibility to fulfill payment and tender documents on behalf of both parties[1]. Remittance and collection belong to commercial credit, in which the buyer is responsible for making payment, with the seller handing over documents.[2]

L/C is a generally adopted term of payment because it provides security of payment to the exporter and enables the buyer to ensure that he receives the goods as ordered and delivered in the way he requires[3]. Specifically, it is an arrangement whereby the buyer requires his bank to establish a credit in favor of the seller[4].

In remittance, there are four parties involved: the remitter, the payee, the remitting bank and paying bank. It can be made by mail, telegraph and draft, namely mail transfer or M/T, telegraphic transfer or T/T and demand draft or D/D.[5]

Collection is of two types: clean collection and documentary collection.[6] Depending on procedure for the issue of documents the payments are grouped into the following types.

Document against payment or D/P[7]—the documents are handed over to the buyer against immediate payment. It can be further divided into D/P at sight and D/P after sight[8]. Document against acceptance or D/A[9]—the documents are handed over to the buyer when the buyer has assumed liability to pay for goods by the date specified in the Usance Bill.[10]

Notes

(1) L/C belongs to banker's credit, which means it is the banker's responsibility to fulfill payment and tender documents on behalf of both parties.

信用证属于银行信用,即银行代替买卖双方负责付款和提交单据。

(2) Remittance and collection belong to commercial credit, in which the buyer is responsible for making payment, with the seller handing over documents.

汇付和托收属于商业信用,买方负责付款,卖方负责提交装船单据。

(3) L/C is a generally adopted term of payment because it provides security of payment to the exporter and enables the buyer to ensure that he receives the goods as ordered and delivered in the way he requires.

信用证是应用较广泛的付款方式,因为它在保证卖方收到款项的同时,也保证买方获得符合其订购和运输要求的货物。

(4) Specifically, it is an arrangement whereby the buyer requires his bank to establish a credit in favor of the seller.

具体来讲,在信用证方式下,买方要求其所在地银行提供以卖方为受益人的信用保证。

(5) It can be made by mail, telegraph and draft, namely mail transfer or M/T, telegraphic transfer or T/T and demand draft or D/D.

汇付可以通过邮件、电传和汇票,即信汇、电汇和票汇实现。

(6) clean collection and documentary collection: 光票托收和跟单托收

(7) Document against payment or D/P: 付款交单

(8) D/P at sight and D/P after sight: 即期付款交单和远期付款交单

(9) Document against acceptance or D/A: 承兑交单

(10) Documents are handed over to the buyer when the buyer has assumed liability to pay for goods by the date specified in the Usance Bill.

出口人的交单以进口人在卖方开出的远期汇票上承兑为条件。

Tips

Anchoring Technique in Negotiation
拴住对方的技巧

Effective negotiators skillfully influence the partner's perceptions of the set of possible outcomes, the Zone of Possible Agreement (ZOPA 协议空间). When deftly used, the opening offer serves as an anchor, often dramatically changing the partner's perception of your reservation price and hence the ZOPA.

The following is an example: Mary and Bob are negotiating over the sale of an automobile. Mary, the seller, is willing to take anything over \$1000. Bob, the potential buyer, is unwilling to pay over \$1500 for the car. Of course, both Mary and Bob know their reservation or walk-away prices, \$1000 and \$1500 respectively, but are uncertain about the partner's walk-away price. Thus neither party knows that any deal in which Bob buys, the care for between \$1000 and \$1500 is better for both parties than no deal.

Bob asks Mary to make the first offer. Mary guesses that Bob is willing to pay at least \$1250 for the car, and may be willing to pay as much as \$1750. She does not want to make an offer that is too outrageously high, since Bob might be insulted and walks away from the deal altogether. Thus, she offers to sell Bob the car for \$1600.

Prior to the first offer, Bob had not thought much about Mary's walk-away price. Bob is thrown off by Mary's offer, only \$100 higher than his walk-away price, and uncertain how to proceed. After a little thought, Bob guesses that Mary's reservation is somewhere around \$1500. All of a sudden, there is a possibility that Bob and Mary might be unable to agree on a deal. Bob tentatively counters with \$1350.

The bargaining continues: Mary counters with $1500. Bob counters with $1400, and Mary offers to "split the difference"(双方各让一半): $1450. Bob accepts and is happy.

（张立玉，邓之宇，石定乐. 商务谈判英语[M]. 武汉：武汉大学出版社，2009：153-154.）

Negotiation Examples

1

A: Hello. You are Mr. Han, aren't you? I'm Liu Qin. Although this is the first time we meet, we know about each other through correspondence[1].

B: Yes, Mr. Liu. It is a great honor[2] to meet you face-to-face today.

A: I'm certain your visit will be fruitful and our talks will contribute[3] a lot to the settling of the payment problem[4].

B: Sure, the payment problem concerns both of us[5]. We have the great intention[6] to cooperate with you to the maximum[7].

A: Well, have you got any specific proposals[8] to make on payment?

B: We propose that your company apply to the Chase Manhattan Bank, New York, USA for a long-term loan[9]. Six months before each shipment, you, through the Chase Manhattan Bank, open, in our favor, an irrevocable, divisible L/C which is to remain valid for three months[10].

A: I'm afraid your proposal is not realistic[11]. Just suppose the Chase Bank agrees to grant us a loan[12], allows us to open an L/C in your favor[13], it seems we're opening an account with the Chase Bank.

B: Yes. As soon as the Chase Bank grants you a loan, it's the same as if you deposited the loan[14] in that bank.

A: That won't do. Our present regulations for controlling foreign exchange do not allow individual enterprises to put money in foreign banks outside China[15]. Besides, the value involved in the transaction is so large that both interest and bank charge for L/C must also be great, which will certainly increase the cost of the project[16].

B: Well, do you have any suggestions?

A: What about payment by installment[17]?

B: In that case, more of our money will be tied up and the price should include this factor[18]. Besides, I think a guarantee from a bank covering the payment is necessary[19].

A: Of course, the factor of more money being tied up should be taken into consideration in pricing[20], and we can ask the Bank of China to give some kind of guarantee.

B：All right. A guarantee from the Bank of China will do.

Notes

（1）correspondence：通信

（2）honor：荣幸

（3）contribute：有助于

（4）the settling of the payment problem：付款问题的解决

（5）concerns both of us：双方都关心

（6）intention：愿意

（7）cooperate with you to the maximum：尽最大的努力与贵方合作

（8）got any specific proposals：有具体的想法

（9）apply to the Chase Manhattan Bank，New York，USA for a long-term loan：向美国纽约大通银行申请长期贷款

（10）Six months before each shipment，you，through the Chase Manhattan Bank，open，in our favor，an irrevocable，divisible L/C which is to remain valid for three months.

每批货装运前6个月，您方通过大通银行向我们开立有效期为三个月的不可撤销的、可分割的信用证。

（11）realistic：现实的

（12）grant us a loan：给我们公司贷款

（13）allows us to open an L/C in your favor：同意我们要求该行向您方开证

（14）deposited the loan：存贷款

（15）Our present regulations for controlling foreign exchange do not allow individual enterprises to put money in foreign banks outside China.

我国现行外汇管理制度还不允许企业在国外银行有存款。

（16）The value involved in the transaction is so large that both interest and bank charge for L/C must also be great，which will certainly increase the cost of the project.

此笔交易金额又那么大，涉及的贷款利息、开证费用都很大，对工程造价将有很大影响。

（17）payment by installment：分期付款

（18）More of our money will be tied up and the price should include this factor.

我们需要投放的资金就更多，那在价格上就应该考虑这一因素。

（19）Guarantee from a bank covering the payment is necessary.

需要有一家银行担保付款才行。

（20）The factor of more money being tied up should be taken into consideration in pricing.

当然在价格上可以考虑你方投放更多资金的因素。

2

A: Now what about the terms of payment?

B: Mr. Wu, we only accept payment by irrevocable L/C payable against shipping documents[1]. It's adopted universally in the international trade[2].

A: Mr. Liu, it's expensive to open an L/C[3]. Besides, we need to put a deposit in the bank, thus tying up the capital of a small company like ours[4]. Could we adopt D/A or D/P[5]?

B: I'm sorry, we can't make an exception[6]. As I've said, we can't accept any other terms of payment. Furthermore, our shoes enjoy a good reputation[7] in oversea markets. The products you are interested in are in great demand and sell especially well[8]. I assure you the quick turnover will offset you L/C expenses and give you a considerable profit[9].

A: As far as I know, you do sometimes accommodate your customers by accepting D/P or D/A.

B: Yes, but only under very unusual circumstances[10].

A: Don't you think ours is a special case?

B: In order to finalize business, we agree to use payment by D/P at sight[11].

A: Could you do me a favor and accept D/P after sight[12]?

B: I'm afraid not. But we will try to make delivery one month earlier.

A: Good. If you promise to effect shipment[13] one month earlier, we will agree to use D/P at sight. Since we have agreed to adopt D/P at sight, the documents will be checked and paid immediately after we receive them[14]. However, we will beg your pardon for refusal of payment in case the papers are not in conformity with the contract[15].

B: We advocate fair play[16]. Of course, payment might be refused if anything goes wrong with the documents. But in that case you must give all the reasons for refusal to the bank once and for all[17]. Mind you, only one refusal of payment is acceptable to the bank. Two or more refusals are not acceptable. Furthermore, please note that you ought to pay us the bank interest once payment is wrongly refused[18].

Notes

(1) We only accept payment by irrevocable L/C payable against shipping documents.

我们只接受不可撤销的信用证条件,根据运输单证支付。

(2) It's adopted universally in the international trade.

在国际贸易中普遍采用这种付款方式。

(3) It's expensive to open an L/C.
开立信用证费用很高。

(4) We need to put a deposit in the bank, thus tying up the capital of a small company like ours.
我们还得向银行交押金,那么像我们这样的小公司资金就无法流动。

(5) Could we adopt D/A or D/P?
能采用付款交单或者承兑交单吗?

(6) We can't make an exception.
我们不能提供例外。

(7) enjoy a good reputation:享有盛誉

(8) are in great demand and sell especially well:需求量很大,销售特别火

(9) I assure you the quick turnover will offset you L/C expenses and give you a considerable profit.
请放心,快速的资金周转会抵消你们的信用证开支,并给你们带来可观的利润。

(10) under very unusual circumstances:在非常特殊的情况下

(11) use payment by D/P at sight:用即期付款交单方式付款

(12) accept D/P after sight:接受远期付款交单方式付款

(13) promise to effect shipment:答应执行装运

(14) The documents will be checked and paid immediately after we receive them.
我们一收到各种单证,就会进行核实并付款。

(15) We will beg your pardon for refusal of payment in case the papers are not in conformity with the contract.
如果各种单证与合同规定不符合,我们会拒付,这可就要请你原谅了。

(16) We advocate fair play.
我们主张公平交易。

(17) In that case you must give all the reasons for refusal to the bank once and for all.
在此种情况下,你必须一次向银行阐明所有拒付的理由。

(18) Please note that you ought to pay us the bank interest once payment is wrongly refused.
请注意,一旦拒付失误,你们要向我方支付银行利息。

Word Bank

5% plus or minus　增减 5%

remittance　汇款

open account 赊账销售、先货后款
cash in advance 预先付款、先款后货
documentary credit or (L/C) 跟单信用证
documentary collection 跟单托收
consignment 寄售业务
advising bank 通知行
issuing bank 开证行
confirming bank 保兑行
negotiation bank 议付行
remitting bank 托收行
collecting bank 代收行
presenting bank 提示行
accepting bank 承兑行
D/P (at sight and after sight) 付款交单(即期和远期)
D/A 承兑交单
standby credit 备用信用证
revolving credit 循环信用证
reciprocal credit 对开信用证
revocable credit 可撤销信用证
transferable credit 可转让信用证
banker's acceptance 银行承兑汇票
B/L(bill of lading) 提单
bill of exchange (draft) 汇票
sight draft 即期汇票
endorsement 背书
freely negotiable L/C 自由议付信用证
UCP 跟单信用证统一惯例
URC 托收统一规则
trial order/try-out order 分期付款
payment by installments 定金
down payment 预付定金
cash settlement 现金结算

Useful Sentences

(1) At what time can we work out a deal?

我们什么时候洽谈生意?

(2) If you insist, we have to stress that these payment terms are very important to us.

我们必须强调这些付款条件对我们很重要。

(3) If you fail to open the L/C within the time, we shall have the right to terminate the contract.

如果你方未能在限定时间内开立信用证,我方有权终止合同。

(4) As agreed upon, you will pay us for the whole set of machine after one-year successful operation of your machine.

经双方同意,在你方设备成功运行一年后再付给我们整套设备款项。

(5) For small orders, we'd like to make the payment by mail transfer after receipt of the documents.

对于小额订单,我们希望在收到单证后以信汇方式支出。

(6) Now that we've settled the price, we can go on to the terms of payment.

既然我们已经解决了价格问题,我们继续谈判付款条件吧。

(7) We'd like to make a down payment first, and then after the delivery, we pay off the rest in four payments in accordance with the progress of the project installation.

我方希望先付定金,其余款项在发货后根据项目安排进展情况分 4 次付清。

(8) I wonder if we can make payment for this order by documentary collection.

我想能否以跟单托收方式支付这次订单。

(9) In terms of installment and deferred payment, the interest rates we charge are the same.

在分期付款和延期付款上,我们对客户加收的利率是一样的。

(10) Please note that our terms of payment are by irrevocable L/C, payable by sight draft accompanied by shipping documents at the Bank of China at the port of shipment.

请注意,我们的付款方式是不可撤销的信用证,凭即期汇票连同装运文件到装运港的中国银行就可支付的信用证。

(11) When payment is to be made by installments, your bank should either give one letter of guarantee for separate installments, or give a separate letter of guarantee for separate installments. Either way, the letter of guarantee should reach us two months before shipment is due.

用分期付款方式付款时,你方银行可以为这一整笔交易写一封担保函,或者分别为每一批货写一封担保函。无论用哪种,这保证函必须在装运前两个月到达我方。

(12) We are eager to know when you can open the relative L/C as we have already bought the goods you required from the mill.

我们急于了解你方何时开立信用证,因我们已经从工厂购来你方所需产品。

(13) We're a small firm of moderate means, and we will not be in a position to execute your order if you don't make half of invoice value as the advance payment.

我们是一家资金有限的小公司,如果你方不能付发票所开价款的一半作为预付款,我们将无法执行订单。

(14) As far as the seller's benefit is concerned, L/C is better than collection, and collection is better than remittance. When collection is adopted, D/P at sight is better than D/P after sight, whereas D/P is better than D/A.

就卖方的利益来说,信用证比托收好,托收又比汇付好。在采用托收方式时,见票即付交单比见票后付款交单好,而付款交单又比承兑交单好。

(15) To guarantee the punctual delivery on the part of the seller and payment by the buyer, different modes of payments have been created, which can be divided into three categories, illustrated as follows: remittance, collection, letter of credit.

为保证卖方能及时交货和买方及时付款,因而产生了几种不同的支付方式。这些方式可分以下三大类: 汇付,托收,信用证。

Tactics for Success

Do You Have a "Good" Agreement?

Is there a preamble in which the intent of the agreement is spelled out clearly?

Are all the issues of interest to all parties addressed?

Are all the proposals workable?

Have all parties affected by the agreement been consulted?

For each point of agreement, is it crystal clear what you have agreed to, including what is to be done, by whom, by what time, and how?

Does the agreement make sense in total?

Is the agreement reasonable and equitable?

Have you considered the major barriers to fulfilling the agreement?

Do you have a vehicle for managing disagreements arising out of this agreement? Is it clear to all parties what this vehicle is and how to use it?

(Roy J Lewicki, Bruce Barry, David M Saunders. 谈判学精要[M]. 大连: 东北财经大学出版社, 2008:109.)

Exercises

Ⅰ. Translate the following words and phrases

D/P (at sight and after sight)
D/A
advising bank
issuing bank
sight draft
terms of payment
the validity period
accept payment
adopt a flexible mode of payment
amend the L/C
立即付款
预付款
其余
分期付款方式
文件
不可撤销的
资助,支持
汇付
托收
信用证

Ⅱ. Translate the following sentences

(1) Unless I receive your remittance within the next three days, our attorney will be instructed to start proceedings to recover the payment.

(2) Owing to unforeseen difficulties encountered by our manufacturers, we find it impossible to effect shipment by the end of this month and would appreciate your extending the shipment date and validity of your L/C to 15th and 30th December respectively.

(3) We have instructed the Bank of China, Beijing to open an irrevocable L/C for $5000 in your favor, valid until November 5.

(4) 我们想知道我们的20号汇票被拒付的原因。

(5) 我们应该在合同中加上货币条款以解决汇率波动问题。

Do You Know

How to Improve Communication in Negotiation Questions for Tough Situations

The Situation	Possible Questions
"Take it or leave it" ultimatums	"If we can come up with a more attractive alternative than that, would you still want me to 'take or leave' your offer?" "Do I have to decide now, or do I have some time to think about it?" "Are you feeling the pressure to bring the negotiation to a close?"
Pressure to respond to an unreasonable deadline	"Why can't we negotiate about this deadline?" "If you're under pressure to meet this deadline, what can I do to help remove some of that pressure?" "What's magical about this afternoon? What about the first thing in the morning?"
Highball or lowball tactics	"What's your reasoning behind this position?" "What would you think I see as a fair offer?" "What standards do you think the final resolution should meet?"
An impasse	"What else can either of us do to close the gap between our positions?" "Specifically what concession do you need from me to bring this to a close right now?" "If it were already six weeks from now and we were looking back at this negotiation, what might we wish we had brought to the table?"
Indecision between accepting and rejecting a proposal	"What's your best alternative to accepting my offer right now?" "If you reject this offer, what will take its place that's better than what you know you'll receive from me?" "How can you be sure that you will get a better deal elsewhere?"
A question about whether the offer you just made is the same as that was offered to others	"What do you see as a fair offer, and given that, what do you think of my current offer to you?" "Do you believe that I think it's in my best interest to be unfair to you?" "Do you believe that people can be treated differently, but still all be treated fairly?"
Attempts to pressure, control, or manipulate	"Shouldn't we both walk away from this negotiation feeling satisfied?" "How would you feel if your roles were reverse, and you were feeling the pressure I'm feeling right now?" "Are you experiencing outside pressures to conclude these negotiations?"

(Sam Deep, Lyle Sussman. What to Ask When You Don't Know What to Say[M]. Upper Saddle River: Prentice Hall, 1993.)

Chapter 8 Negotiations on Packing

第 8 章 包装的谈判

Lead-in

Proper packing can be very critical based on the type of product and its destination. Before goods are packed, exporters should consider the purpose of the packing. Various factors influence types of cargo packing for international consignments.

Learning Objectives

In this chapter, you will be able to:

- Know about the negotiations on packing.
- Know about the strategy of negotiations on packing.

Proper packing can be extremely important based on the type of product and its destination. Exporters should take the following reasons into consideration.

(1) Strong packing can prevent the goods from being stolen and damaged.

(2) Reasonable packing can lessen shipping space and save freight.

(3) It is convenient for goods to be stored, taken care of, transported, loaded and calculated with appropriate packing.

(4) Good packing can ensure the lowest insurance premium.

(5) Marketing packing enables the consumers to select, carry or use the goods with convenience.

(6) Marketing packing can beautify the commodity, attract consumers, expand sales and increase gains on foreign exchanges as well.

The following factors should be paid attention to.

(1) Packing should be in compliance with customs or statutory requirements.[1]

(2) Packing must meet insurance acceptance conditions.

(3) General merchandises require adequate packing of various types, such as fruit in cartons, chemicals in bags and electrical equipment in wooden cases.[2]

Packing can be divided into transport packing (outer packing) and sales packing (inner packing). Transport packing should be solid and durable, adaptable to the changing climates during the long journey, convenient for storage, stowing, calculation, cargo inspection and identification, and have the least weight, volume and cost.[3]

Transport packing consists of transport marks, directive marks and warning marks.[4] Transport marks includes: consignor's or consignee's code name, the number of the contract or the L/C, the port of destination, number of the packed goods, weight and dimensions.[5] Directive marks are composed of eye-catching figures and concise instructions regarding manner of proper handling, storing, loading and unloading of the packed goods, e. g. KEEP DRY.[6] Warning marks are obvious symbols or words to warn people against the hidden danger of inflammables, explosives and poisonous products, e. g. Toxic and Infectious Substances.[7]

Sales packing can help to increase sales of goods. It is regarded as "the silent salesman".[8] Neutral packing carries no mark and name of the origin country of the packed goods and no sign of the original trademark so as to elude the tariff of the import country or satisfy the buyer's special requirement.[9]

Notes

(1) Packing should be in compliance with customs or statutory requirements.

包装应符合海关要求或有关法律的规定。

(2) General merchandises require adequate packing of various types, such as fruit on cartons, chemicals in bags and electrical equipment in wooden cases.

常规商品根据不同类型采用不同的包装,如水果用纸箱,化工产品用袋装,电气设备则使用木箱。

(3) Transport packing should be solid and durable, adaptable to the changing climates during the long journey, convenient for storage, stowing, calculation, cargo inspection and identification, and have the least weight, volume and cost.

运输包装应坚固、耐用,能够适应长途运输途中的各种气候,方便货物的仓储、堆放、计算、商检和识别。包装应尽可能做到体积小、重量轻和费用低。

(4) Transport packing consists of transport marks, directive marks and warning marks.

运输包装上应标明运输标志、指示性标志和警告性标志。

(5) Transport marks includes: consignor's or consignee's code name, the number of the contract or the L/C, the port of destination, number of the packed good, weight and dimensions.

运输标志包括发货人或收货人的代号、合同号或信用证号、目的港名称、货物件数、重量与体积等内容。

(6) Directive marks are composed of eye-catching figures and concise instructions regarding manner of proper handling, storing, loading and unloading of the packed goods, e. g. KEEP DRY.

指示性标志提示人们在搬运、仓储、装卸过程中需要注意的事项,一般都是以简单醒目的图形和文字在包装上标出。例如,防潮。

(7) Warning marks are obvious symbols or words to warn people against the hidden danger of inflammables, explosives and poisonous products, e. g. Toxic and Infectious Substances.

警告性标志:凡在运输包装内装有易燃物品、爆炸品、有毒物品等危险货物时,都必须在运输包装上标明用于各种危险品的标志,以示警告。例如,有毒和有传染性的物品。

(8) Sales packing can help to increase sales of goods. It is regarded as "the silent salesman".

销售包装有促销的功能。它也被称为"无声的推销员"。

(9) Neutral packing carries no mark and name of the origin country of the packed goods and no sign of the original trademark so as to elude the tariff of the import country or satisfy the buyer's special requirement.

中性包装指的是既不标明生产地名,也无商标,以打破某些进口国家的关税壁垒以及适应买家的特殊需要。

Traps to Avoid

Good Guy/Bad Guy Routine

This "good guy/bad buy" tactic is similar to the good cop/bad cop routine portrayed in many police dramas in which a person is questioned by two detectives—one who acts tough, uses foul language, threatens the person, and then leaves the room, while the other expresses sympathy and offers assistance if the person cooperates before the "bad" cop returns. In negotiation situations, the classic case is a husband and wife looking to buy a house. The husband could, for example, tell the owner all the things he loves about the house, but also confide that his wife has a few reservations and is not certain that they can't find one more to her liking—if they don't buy this house quickly and at a good price. Whether or not that is in reality the case, the owner is likely at least to partially believe it, and therefore may accept the buyers' offer or make a counteroffer.

(Peter B Stark, Jane Flaherty. The Only Negotiating Guide You'll Ever Need[M]. New York: Broadway Books, 2003: 170.)

Negotiation Examples

1

A: Mr. Zhou, shall we now discuss about the packing?

B: Very well. You know, we have definite ways of packing garments. [1] As to hats, we use a polythene wrapper for each article, all ready for window display[2].

A: Good. A wrapping that catches the eye will certainly help push the sales[3]. With competition from similar garment producers, the merchandise must not only be of good value but also look attractive. [4]

B: Right you are. We'll see to it that the hats appeal to the eye as well as to the purse. [5]

A: What about the outer packing?

B: We'll pack them 8 dozen to one carton, gross weight around 15 kilos a carton.

A: Cartons?

B: Yes, corrugated cardboard boxes.

A: Could you use wooden cases instead?

B: Why use wooden cases?

A: I'm afraid the cardboard boxes are not strong enough for such a heavy load. [6]

B: The cartons are comparatively light, and therefore easy to handle. [7] They won't be stowed away with the heavy cargo. [8] The stevedores will see to that. Besides, we'll reinforce the cartons with straps. [9] Hats are not fragile goods. [10] They can stand a lot of jolting.

A: Maybe you're right, but the goods are to be transshipped at Hamburg or London. If the boxes are moved about on an open wharf, the dampness or rain may get into them. This would make the hat spotted or ruined.

B: No need to worry about that. The cartons lined with plastic sheets are water-proof, and as the boxes are made of cardboard, they will be handled with care. [11]

A: Well, I don't want to take any chances. Besides, cartons are easy to cut open and this increases the risk of pilferage.

B: Tampering with cartons is easily detected.[12] I should say that this rather discourages pilferage.[13]

A: Maybe so, but I'm afraid that in case of damage or pilferage, the insurance company will refuse compensation on the ground of improper packing, or packing unsuitable for sea voyage.[14]

B: But cartons are quite seaworthy. They are widely used in our shipments to continental ports. There are no complaints from our clients, and such packing has also been approved by our insurance company for W. P. A. and T. P. N. D.

A: If you could guarantee compensation in case the insurance company refuses to honor a claim for faulty packing, we would be quite willing to accept cartons.

B: I'm sorry, but we can't take on any responsibility for every kind of mishap.[15]

A: I understand your position. Perhaps we have demanded too much.

B: If you insist, we'll use wooden cases, but the charge for packing will be much higher, and it also slows down the delivery.

A: Well, I'll cable home immediately for instructions on the matter.

B: OK. I'll be waiting for your reply.

Notes

(1) You know, we have definite ways of packing garments.

您知道,我们有专门包装服装的方法。

(2) As to hats, we use a polythene wrapper for each article, all ready for window display.

至于帽子,我们用聚乙烯封套,可以放到橱窗展示。

(3) A wrapping that catches the eye will certainly help push the sales.

好的包装可以吸引眼球,并促进销售。

(4) With competition from similar garment producers, the merchandise must not only be of good value but also look attractive.

由于有类似服装生产者的竞争,产品不仅要质量好,而且要美观。

(5) We'll see to it that the hats appeal to the eye as well as to the purse.

我们要保证帽子物美价廉。

(6) I'm afraid the cardboard boxes are not strong enough for such a heavy load.

我担心硬纸盒不够结实,不能放这样重的东西。

(7) The cartons are comparatively light, and therefore easy to handle.

纸板箱相对轻,好搬好放。

(8) They won't be stowed away with the heavy cargo.

它们不能承受重物。

(9) The stevedores will see to that. Besides, we'll reinforce the cartons with straps.

装运工将会注意的。而且,我们还会用铁皮带加固。

(10) Hats are not fragile goods.

帽子不是易碎物品。

(11) The cartons lined with plastic sheets are water-proof, and as the boxes are made of cardboard, they will be handled with care.

硬纸盒用塑料包上,可以防水,而且盒子是硬纸盒的,可以轻拿轻放。

(12) Tampering with cartons is easily detected.

硬纸盒如被损害,很容易被发现。

(13) I should say that this rather discourages pilferage.

应该说这点使得产品不易被盗。

(14) but I'm afraid that in case of damage or pilferage, the insurance company will refuse compensation on the ground of improper packing, or packing unsuitable for sea voyage.

但是我担心一旦有损坏或者被盗,保险公司会以包装不当或不适宜海运为由拒绝理赔。

(15) but we can't take on any responsibility for every kind of mishap.

但是我们不能对任何小问题负责。

2

A: I'm told that some of the goods needn't be packed. What are they?

B: Bulk cargoes and nude cargoes. [1]

A: What are bulk cargoes?

B: Bulk cargoes refer to those such as iron ore, grain, coal which needn't be packed, or it's difficult or even impossible to have them packed. [2]

A: I see. Then what are nude cargoes?

B: Nude cargoes are those with regular shapes and in pieces of different shapes. For example, steel plates, timber and rubber. Besides these, the other cargoes should usually be packed. [3]

A: When considering the outer packing of cargoes, what are factors to consider?

B: Well, in order to save freight cost, packing must be economical, convenient for storing, transporting, loading and unloading. [4] We should bear in mind that reasonable packing can reduce shipping space.

A: How should we pack those goods which will be transshipped on the way?

B: Durable packing materials should be used in order to protect the goods from any possible damage during transit. The packing materials you select should depend on the size, shape, weight, fragility and contents of the goods. [5] Packing should be waterproof and dampproof because the goods might be moved about on an open wharf. [6] We have to be concerned about the possible jolting, squeezing and collision that may take place when the cargoes are moved about. [7]

A: I understand that packing should meet the requirements of different means of transportation. Could you be more specific?

B: Seaworthy packing should be strong and protective against squeezing and bumping while packages for air transportation should be light and compact. [8]

A: I know that the insurance company will refuse to compensate if the goods are improperly packed. [9] Then how do I make sure the goods will be packed well enough?

B: No insurance company can give a hard and fast rule because of the variances in what is shipped. [10] One guideline I can give you is that if the goods can survive a 2-metre fall, it is packed well enough. [11]

Notes

(1) Bulk cargoes and nude cargoes.

散装货物和裸装货物。

(2) Bulk cargoes refer to those such as iron ore, grain, coal which needn't be packed, or it's difficult or even impossible to have them packed.

散装货物有铁矿石、谷类、煤等不需要或很难、甚至不可能包装的产品。

(3) Nude cargoes are those with regular shapes and in pieces of different shapes. For example, steel plates, timber and rubber. Besides these, the other cargoes should usually be packed.

裸装货物指的是那些形状规则以及不同形状的一些碎片。比如钢材、木材、橡胶。除了这些,其他货物均应包装。

(4) in order to save freight cost, packing must be economical, convenient for storing, transporting, loading and unloading.

为了节省运输费,包装必须经济实用,便于仓储、搬动、装卸。

(5) The packing materials you select should depend on the size, shape, weight, fragility and contents of the goods.

包装材料的选择要取决于货物的尺寸、形状、重量、易受损程度和容量。

(6) Packing should be waterproof and dampproof because the goods might be moved about on an open wharf.

由于货物或许会堆放在露天码头,包装必须防水、防潮。

(7) We have to be concerned about the possible jolting, squeezing and collision that may take place when the cargoes are moved about.

我们还要考虑在搬运中货物会受到颠簸、挤压、碰撞。

(8) Seaworthy packing should be strong and protective against squeezing and bumping while packages for air transportation should be light and compact.

适合于海运的包装要坚固、结实,要经受得起挤压和碰撞;适合于空运的包装要轻便、小巧。

(9) I know that the insurance company will refuse to compensate if the goods are improperly packed.

我知道如果货物包装不当,保险公司会拒绝赔偿。

(10) No insurance company can give a hard and fast rule because of the variances in what is shipped.

由于运输货物种类繁多,保险公司不可能有什么硬性的规定。

(11) One guideline I can give you is that if the goods can survive a 2-metre fall, it is packed well enough.

我的方法是:如果货物从两米高处摔下来还能完好无缺,那么包装就可以说是过关的了。

Word Bank

number 个数
net weight 净重
capacity 容积
gross for net 以毛作净
volume 体积
tare 皮重
gross weight 毛重
wooden case 木箱
chest 茶叶箱
crate 板条箱
skeleton case 漏孔箱
carton 纸板箱

sack 布袋
gunny bag 麻袋
bale 包
barrel 琵琶桶
cask 啤酒桶
tub 桶
drum 鼓型桶
glass container 玻璃器皿

Useful Sentences

(1) All bags contain an inner waterproof lining.
所有包内都有一层防水内衬。

(2) The crates are charged to you at $5 each if they are not returned to us within 2 weeks.
如果板条箱两星期内不归还，则每只箱扣罚 5 美元。

(3) Solid packing and overall stuffing can prevent the cases from vibration and jarring.
坚固的木箱和箱内严密的填充可防止木箱受震、开裂。

(4) Those goods are available in strong wooden drums of 1,2,5,10 and 20 litres.
这些货物分别装入 1 升、2 升、5 升、10 升、20 升的木桶里。

(5) Fifty-litre carboy would be the most economical size. Carboys may be retained without charge for two months.
50 升的瓶子应是最经济的尺码，这些瓶子可免费保存两个月。

(6) The various items of your order will be packed into bundles of suitable sizes for shipment.
你们订单上的各种货物被打成各种大小不同的捆儿，以便于运输。

(7) Please keep the cartons to 15kg each and metal-strap all cartons in stacks of 4.
请将每个纸箱重量限制在 15 公斤内，并将每 4 箱一组用铁条儿固定起来。

(8) Each item is to be wrapped separately in gerase-paper.
每件货物应单独用油纸包好。

(9) All measurements of each case must not exceed 1.5m × 1m × 1m.
每只木箱体积不应超过 1.5m × 1m × 1m。

(10) Each single crate is heavily padded and packed with 4 carboys.
每只板条箱内装 4 只大瓶子将空余处填满。

(11) Full details regarding packing and marking must be strictly observed.
请严格遵守包装及商标的细则。

(12) To facilitate carrying, rope or metal handles are indispensable and should be fixed to the boxes.

为便于搬运,绳子或铁把手不可缺少,并将其固定在箱子上。

(13) Our packing charge includes \$1 for the drum, which sum will be credited on return.

包装费中有1美元是包装桶的费用,此费用在桶还给我们时可退回。

(14) The whole carton is packed with double straps, each corner of the carton consolidated with metal angles.

纸箱外加了两道箍,每个箱角都用金属角加固。

(15) Foam plastics are applied to protect the goods against press.

泡沫塑料用来防止货物被挤压。

Tips

Requirements for Packing

To stand long transportation of the ocean and rough handling of cargoes, and for other purposes, the outer packing of the cargoes should meet the following requirements: be solid and durable, adaptable to the changing climates at the loading and unloading ports; be uniform so as to convenience storage, stowing, calculation, cargo inspection and identification: have the least weight, volume, and cost increase. As packing materials, wood must be disinfected and many countries forbid straw to be used for the packing of imported goods.

(Roy J. Lewicki, Bruce Barry, David M. Saunders. Essentials of Negotiation. Dalian: Dongbei University of Finance & Economics Press, 2008.)

(浩瀚. 商务英语谈判高频话题[M]. 北京: 中国水利水电出版社,2009:131.)

Exercises

Ⅰ. Translate the following words and phrases

measurement
the ordinal number of package
insecure packing
protect the goods against
examined by customs
protect against dampness, moisture, rust and shock

solid packing and overall stuffing
reinforce the packing
2 to 3 dozens
foam-plastics
包装费
内包装
外包装
设计
独特的风格
木箱
唛头
标明
损坏
纸盒

Ⅱ. Translate the following sentences

(1) We have already taken steps to improve our packing and I'm sure our future shipments will give your clients satisfaction.

(2) The cigars are packed 5 pieces to a small packet, 20 packets to a carton, 144 cartons to a cardboard container.

(3) The German or Dutch description of the current labels is to be deleted.

(4) 请注意箱子外面要注明"易碎品"及"小心轻放"的标记。

(5) 请注意包装要经得起长途海运。

Do You Know

Negotiation Planning Guide

(1) What are the issues in the upcoming negotiation?

(2) Based on a review of ALL the issues, what is the "bargaining mix"? (Which issues do we have to cover? Which issues are connected to other issues?)

(3) What are my interests?

(4) What are my limits—what is my walk-away price? What is my alternative?

(5) Defining targets and openings—where will I start, what is my goal?

(6) Who are my constituents and what do they want me to do?

(7) Who are the opposing negotiators and what do they want?

(8) What overall strategy do I want to select?

(9) What protocol needs to be followed in conducting this negotiation?

(Roy J Lewicki, Bruce Barry, David M Saunders. 谈判学精要[M]. 大连：东北财经大学出版社，2008.)

Chapter 9　Negotiations on Insurance

第 9 章　保险的谈判

Lead-in

Insurance is a contract whereby the insurer, on the basis of a premium paid, undertakes to indemnify the insured against loss at certain risks or perils to which the cargo insured may be exposed.

Learning Objectives

In this chapter, you will be able to:

- Know about the negotiations on insurance.
- Know about the strategy of negotiations on insurance.

At present, according to the different transportation methods, there are ocean marine transportation insurance, overland transportation insurance, air transportation insurance and parcel post transportation insurance in our country.[1] Among all these, ocean marine transportation insurance is most widely used in international trade practical business, which is also the first used insurance among the all. The overland and air transportation insurances have developed on the basis of the ocean insurance. Even though they have different obligations, their basic principles and guarantees provided by the insurance companies are nearly the same.

In marine cargo transport insurance, risks fall into the following kinds.

(1) Perils of the sea (海上风险)

Natural calamity(自然灾害,the perils under force majeure such as vile weather, thunder storm and lightening, earthquake, flood, etc.).

Fortuitous accidents(意外事故,risks such as ship stranding, striking upon the rocks, ship sinking, ship collision, fire, explosion, etc.).

(2) Extraneous risks(外来风险)

General extraneous risks(一般外来风险,risks caused by theft, rain, leakage, shortage, dampness, heating, hooking, rusting, etc.).

Special extraneous risks(特殊外来风险,risks caused by war, strikes, failure of delivery and rejection, etc.).

The losses and damages done to the goods can fall into the following kinds.

(1) Total loss(全部损失)

Actual total loss(实际全损,the whole lot of the consignment has been lost or damaged or found valueless upon the arrival at the port of destination).

Constructive total loss(推定全损,The actual loss of the insured goods is unavoidable, or the ship or the consignment has to be abandoned because the cost of salvage or recovery would exceed the value of the ship and the consignment in sound condition upon the arrival of the port of destination).

Most insurance policies provide for the payment of a total loss up to the insured amount.[2]

(2) Partial loss(部分损失)

General average (G. A. 共同海损,When both the ship and the consignments on board are engaged and the captain, for the safety of the ship and the consignments, intentionally and reasonably does some sacrifices or makes some expenses).

Particular average (P. A. 单独海损,a particular consignment is partially damaged).

Ocean cargo insurance also covers the expenses incurred to avoid or reduce the damage to or loss of the subject matter insured, which falls into the following kinds[3].

Sue and labor expenses(施救费用,made by the insured or his agent to prevent them from suffering further losses).

Salvage charges(救助费用,made to those other than the insured, the carrier and the insurer who come to the salvage of the ship and the consignments).

Notes

(1) At present, according to the different transportation methods, there are ocean marine transportation insurance, overland transportation insurance, air transportation insurance and

parcel post transportation insurance in our country.

目前,我国办理的进出口货物运输保险业务按照运输方式不同,主要分为海洋运输货物保险、陆上运输货物保险、航空运输货物保险和邮包运输保险等。

(2) Most insurance policies provide for the payment of a total loss up to the insured amount.

大多数的保单中规定赔偿损失的总金额最多可达到所投保的金额。

(3) Ocean cargo insurance also covers the expenses incurred to avoid or reduce the damage to or loss of the subject matter insured, which falls into the following kinds.

海上货物保险也包括为避免或减少被保货物的损坏或损失所支出的费用,主要有以下几种。

Tips

Framing Technique in Negotiation
(以退为进,给谈判定下基调的技巧)

The following dialogue is based on an actual conversation between a seller's agent and a buyer. A three-bedroom house was put on the market for $170 000. The buyer opened with an offer of $155 000. In response, the seller demanded $165 000, to which the buyer responded with $157 000. The seller countered with $164 000. At that point, the buyer, a bit frustrated by the "negotiation dance(谈判耍的花招)", offered to "split the difference": $160 500. The seller rejected the offer, countering with a demand of $163 000. It is at this point that we resume the conversation between the seller's agent and the buyer.

BUYER: So, did the seller accept my offer?

SELLER'S AGENT: No, I'm sorry. The seller countered with $163 000.

BUYER: $163 000? I can't believe she rejected my offer. Is she crazy? I made a very fair offer to split the difference and she only comes down by $1000? What's going on?

SELLER AGENT: Let me try to explain what I think is going on. The seller paid over $200 000 for the property. She knows that she can't sell the house for that much, but still every dollar really hurts her. On the other hand, the two of you are only $2500 apart. She probably figures that an extra $2500 to you is just another $19.56 per month for a 30-year mortgage at 8.5% interest.

BUYER: It's true that $2500 is just an extra $19.56 per month, but $2500 is still TWO THOUSAND AND FIVE HUNDRED DOLLARS! You try to tell me that $2500 isn't a lot of money! Think of all the furniture I can buy for that much money. And if I pay an extra $2500 now, that's an extra $2500 I have to get back when I furnish the house.

Both the buyer and the seller are engaging in what might be called framing. Framing is used to emphasize the value of their concession; to provide a justification for the partner to make concessions; and to offer a standard of fairness for dividing the value created by negotiating.

（张立玉，邓之宇，石定乐. 商务谈判英语[M]. 武汉：武汉大学出版社，2009：153-154.）

Negotiation Examples

1

A: What is the primary purpose of insurance?

B: It protects against damage to or loss of goods during shipping[1].

A: A business acquaintance told me that you are an experienced exporter. Why don't you explain how goods are valued for insurance purposes? I suppose there is more than one factor that goes to make up insured valuation.[2]

B: Yes, the primary factor is the cost of the goods at the point of delivery.[3] Then, too, it depends on whether goods are shipped FOB or EX-factory.[4]

A: I'd like to hear something about those unfamiliar terms.

B: FOB means free on board. This means the seller is responsible for delivery of the goods to the carrier, and from there the buyer is responsible. EX-factory means from the point of origin.[5] This means that the buyer pays all shipping costs from the factory.

A: How should we go about shipping the baby coaches?

B: Our firm uses a freight forwarder.[6] As soon as the order is ready, my company issues an order to our freight handler.[7] They prepare all the documents needed for shipping, including the certificate of insurance.

A: I understand freight forwarders handle packing and insurance as well as the other documents needed for export.

B: Right.

A: What sort of documents do you need to provide to the freight forwarders?

B: We must submit a commercial invoice which provides accurate information about the goods, their value, their quantity, and the names of the consignor and consignee.[8]

A: But it's the freight forwarder who chooses the insurance company?

B: Yes, they only deal with reputable firms, so you can be sure of dependable coverage.[9]

A: The insurance is protection against loss arising from damage?

B: Yes, we're usually covered for loss or damage. As soon as the insurance company gets the export declaration—if they agree to insure—they write a policy fixing the terms and the premium.[10]

A: And then the consignee pays the premium?

B: And the insurance company issues a receipt for the premium called a covering note.[11] That secures the goods until the actual policy is written.

A: So from that point on we're protected against loss or damage?

B: Some policies cover TLO, so in that case we're covered for total loss of goods only, not for partial loss or damage. But all this is always spelled out in advance.

A: Well, thanks for the information.

Notes

(1) It protects against damage or loss of goods during shipping.

保障货物在运送途中免受损害或丢失。

(2) I suppose there is more than one factor that goes to make up insured valuation.

我猜构成货物投保价值的因素,一定不止一个。

(3) Primary factor is the cost of the goods at the point of delivery.

主要因素是货物交货成本。

(4) Then, too, it depends on whether goods are shipped FOB or EX-factory.

还有货物是以离岸价还是工厂交货价运输,也是影响投保价值的因素。

(5) EX-factory means from the point of origin.

EX-factory 的意思是工厂交货。

(6) Our firm uses a freight forwarder.

我们公司委托货运公司。

(7) As soon as the order is ready, my company issues an order to our freight handler.

当货备好要运输时,我们会发一张装货单给负责货运的公司。

(8) We must submit a commercial invoice which provides accurate information about the goods, their value, their quantity, and the names of the consignor and consignee.

我们必须出具一份商业发票,标明有关货物名称及价值、货物的数量以及托运人与收货人的准确资料。

(9) They only deal with reputable firms, so you can be sure of dependable coverage.

他们只跟声誉好的公司打交道,所以你大可放心此可靠性。

(10) We're usually covered for loss or damage. As soon as the insurance company gets the export declaration—if they agree to insure—they write a policy fixing the terms and the premium.

通常保的是损失或损害。保险公司一拿到出口报单后——如果他们同意保的话——

他们就会签一张保单，确定保单的条件与保费。

(11) And the insurance company issues a receipt for the premium called a covering note. 保险公司这时候会出一份保费收据，叫做承保通知单。

2

A: Mr. Zhang, does "all marine risks" mean less than "all risks"?[1]

B: It means risks incident to transport by sea, such as collision, stranding, fire, penetration of sea water into the holds of the ships, etc..[2] In other words, under "all marine risks", recoverable loss will only be confined to those arising from perils of the sea and maritime accidents only.[3] The "all risks" coverage will admit all losses occurring at any time throughout the whole currency of the coverage, irrespective of whether they are caused by accidents at sea or on land. In this sense, "all marine risks" provides a more limited cover than "all risks".[4]

A: I see. Another thing I don't understand at this moment is the advantage of W. P. A. coverage. I thought that W. P. A. insurance should cover all principal risks while, according to what you say, it means very little. It seems to be a phrase without much substance.[5] Just what is the difference between W. P. A. and F. P. A.?[6]

B: This is a question which is very often overlooked, Mr. Johnson. It is a very common but mistaken idea that a merchant has done everything that is required to protect him against losses when he has taken out W. P. A. insurance. There is, perhaps, no mistake more detrimental to his interests.[7]

A: This is where my interest lies. I must confess that I was under the impression that W. P. A. insurance was quite sufficient and that losses due to breakage were covered. I know that F. P. A. insurance does not cover losses on consumer goods, but I did think that the W. P. A. insurance covered more risks than the F. P. A.

B: Actually, it is like this. There is some difference between W. P. A. and F. P. A. The F. P. A. clause does not cover partial loss of the nature of particular average, whereas the W. P. A. clause covers such losses when they exceed a prearranged percentage. This is the sole difference between W. P. A. and F. P. A. Otherwise, the protection under the F. P. A. clause will be almost identical with that offered by the W. P. A. clause, because in the event of maritime accidents encountered in transit, such as stranding, fire, explosion or collision, both clauses will cover particular average losses in full.[8]

A: I don't mean to annoy you, Mr. Zhang, but I don't quite grasp this. Couldn't you say it in simpler terms?

B: I'll try. Neither the W. P. A nor the F. P. A. mentions the risks covered or the risks excluded. The extent of insurance is stipulated in the basic policy form and in the various risks clauses.[9] Look at the insurance certificates and you will find that the risks of theft and pilferage, freshwater, oil, grease, hooks, breakage, leakage, contamination, deterioration, etc. are specifically mentioned and must be specifically applied for.[10] These are special risks. F. P. A. stands for "Free from Particular Average".

A: Mr. Zhang, you have corrected my ideas about the insurance. I see now that this is far more complicated than I ever imagined.

B: Now I know why you often point out to us the wording of some letters of credit which you feel fussy about. But what are we to do about it? We must keep to the stipulations of the contract and the letter of credit.

A: The blame does not only rest with the letter of credit. For an item like ceramics, I think the Light Industrial Products Corporation should have understood from our letter of credit that we wanted to cover all risks, including the risk of breakage. I must say the error was on both sides and I think the loss ought to be shared by both parties, let us say half and half.

B: Our price calculation could hardly admit that. Besides, we acted upon your instructions, so it is not our fault. But in view of our good relationship, we'll supply you with a favorable offer to compensate some of your losses.[11]

A: I sincerely hope that you gentlemen will settle that matter to our mutual satisfaction.

Notes

(1) Does "all marine risks" means less than "all risks"?

"一切海洋运输货物险"是否意味着比"一切险"范围窄一些?

(2) It means risks incident to transport by sea, such as collision, stranding, fire, penetration of sea water into the holds of the ships, etc..

"一切海洋运输货物险"意味着海运中的意外风险,诸如船舶碰撞、搁浅、起火、海水侵入船舱等。

(3) In other words, under "all marine risks", recoverable loss will only be confined to those arising from perils of the sea and maritime accidents only.

也就是说,"一切海洋运输货物险",其损失的赔偿只限于因海上灾难和海运意外事故所引起的损失。

(4) The "all risks" coverage will admit all losses occurring at any time throughout the whole currency of the coverage, irrespective of whether they are caused by accidents at sea or on land. In this sense, "all marine risks" provides a more limited cover than "all risks".

而保"一切险"在全部承保期内的任何时间,不论海上或陆上所产生的意外事故,其全部损失都予以赔偿。从这层意义上说，“一切海洋运输货物险”的承保范围较“一切险”有限。

(5) It seems to be a phrase without much substance.

徒有虚名，而没有多少内容。

(6) Just what is the difference between W. P. A. and F. P. A.?

那么“水渍险”和“平安险”有什么区别呢？

(7) It is a very common but mistaken idea that a merchant has done everything that is required to protect him against losses when he has taken out W. P. A. insurance. There is, perhaps, no mistake more detrimental to his interests.

一个很普通但错误的想法，就是商人投保了“水渍险”，便以为足以保障其利益不受损失。恐怕没有别的错误比这个更为有害于他自己的利益的了。

(8) Otherwise, the protection under the F. P. A. clause will be almost identical with that offered by the W. P. A. clause, because in the event of maritime accidents encountered in transit, such as stranding, fire, explosion or collision, both clauses will cover particular average losses in full.

除此以外，“平安险”条款所承保的责任与“水渍险”条款所承保的责任差不多相同。因为万一在运输途中遭遇海上意外事故，诸如搁浅、着火、爆炸或碰撞，这两种条款都全部赔付单独海损的损失。

(9) The extent of insurance is stipulated in the basic policy form and in the various risks clauses.

保险范围是写在基本保险单内和在各种险别条款里。

(10) Look at the insurance certificates and you will find that the risks of theft and pilferage, freshwater, oil, grease, hooks, breakage, leakage, contamination, deterioration, etc. are specifically mentioned and must be specifically applied for.

看一下保险凭证，你将看到对偷窃险、淡水险、油渍险、油污险、钩损险、破碎险、渗漏险、玷污险等都特加说明，必须特别申保，这就是特别险。

(11) But in view of our good relationship, we'll supply you with a favorable offer to compensate some of your losses.

但鉴于我们之间的良好关系，我们准备给你开个优惠报盘，借以补偿一些你方的损失。

Word Bank

consignment 寄售

invitation of tender 招标

submission of tender　投标
agent　一般代理人
general agent　总代理人
agency agreement　代理协议
accumulative commission　累计佣金
compensation trade/compensating/compensatory trade　补偿贸易(或抵偿贸易,往返贸易)
counter trade　对销贸易
processing on giving materials　来料加工
assembling on provided parts　来料装配
exclusive right　独家经营/专营权
exclusivity agreement　独家经营/包销/代理协议
exclusive agent; sole agency; sole agent; exclusive agency　独家代理
consignee　收货人
consigner　发货人
time of delivery　交货时间
time of shipment　装运期限
estimated time of arrival (ETA)　预计到达时间
estimated time of departure (ETD)　预计离开时间
charter (the chartered ship)　租船
voyage charter　定程租船
time charter　定期租船
to postpone delivery/delay in delivery　推迟发货
port of loading/destination　装货港、到岸港
means of conveyance　运输手段、方式

Useful Sentences

(1) I don't think it necessary to tell you that the extra insurance premium will be for your account.

额外的保险费用由你方承担,这我就不必说了吧。

(2) Breakage is a special risk, for which an extra insurance premium will have to be charged.

破碎险是一种特别险,需要收取额外的保险费。

(3) In particular, we hope to know whether you can issue a special rate in return for the

promise of regular monthly shipments.

特别提及的是，我方想知道贵方能否给予一个特别的保险费率，作为我方每月定期发货承诺的回报。

(4) I will have the goods covered against Free from Particular Average.

我将为货物投保平安险。

(5) We are glad to advise you that we have insured your shipment of cotton products, up to value of US $25 000.

本公司高兴地通知贵方，已经将一批棉制品货物投保，总价值为2.5万美元。

(6) Will you please quote your terms for providing the required cover, which should include loading and discharging?

敬请告知贵方客户指定的保险收费条件，包括货物装卸费在内。

(7) Another thing, I'd like to have the insurance of the goods covered at 120% of the invoice value.

此外，我希望这批货物按发票金额的120%来投保。

(8) What coverage can you provide for my consignment?

对于我们这批货物，你们能够为我们投保什么险？

(9) An All Risks insurance covers every sort of hazard, doesn't it?

一份综合险报单保所有的险，不是吗？

(10) You can exercise your rights according to the insurance contract.

你们可以按照保险合同行使自己的权利。

(11) Because you hold the insurance policy, we shall be grateful if you take the matter up for us with the People's Insurance Company of China.

由于保险单在你处，如果你方能为我们向中国人民保险公司投保，我们非常感激。

(12) We can cover various kinds of insurance, including FPA (Free from Particular Average), WPA (With Particular Average), AR (All Risks), TLO (Total Loss Only).

我们可以保各种险别：包括平安险、水渍险、综合险和全损险等。

(13) Insurance rates vary with different types of cargoes and risks.

保险费率根据货物种类和险别的不同而不同。

(14) The term "average" means "loss" in most cases when it comes to insurance business.

在保险业中，average一词指的是"海损"。

(15) Credit insurance is provided by the insurer to compensate of the loss of the creditor when the debtor defaults on payment or refuses to pay.

信用保险是由保险人负责赔偿债权人因债务人不能履行偿付或拒绝偿付时所遭受到的损失的一种保险。

Tactics for Success

Dovetailing—Asking for Their Preference

One way to dovetail interests (让利益相互融合) is to invent several options all equally acceptable to you and ask the partner which one they prefer. You want to know what is preferable, not necessarily what is acceptable. You can then take the option, work with it some more, and again present two or more variants, asking which one they prefer. In this way, without anyone's making a decision, you can improve a plan until you can find no more joint gains. For example, the agent for the baseball star might ask the team owner: "What meets your interest better, a salary of $875 000 a year for four years, or $1 000 000 a year for three years? The latter? OK, how about between that and $900 000 a year for three years with a $500 000 bonus in each year if Fernado pitches better than a 3.00 ERA?"

If dovetailing had to be summed up in one sentence, it would be: Look for items that are of low costs to you and high benefit to them and vice versa. Differences in interests, priorities, beliefs, forecasts, and attitudes towards risk all make dovetailing possible. A negotiator's motto could be "Vivi la difference!"

(张立玉,邓之宇,石定乐. 商务谈判英语[M]. 武汉: 武汉大学出版社,2009:153-154.)

Exercises

Ⅰ. Translate the following words and phrases

marine insurance
contract of indemnity
general average
file
take out cover
inconsistent
on second thoughts leftover
ocean marine cargo insurance
incur
保险合同
保险单
被保险人

保险人
保险费
承担保险
全部损失
部分损失
保险索赔
保险凭证

Ⅱ. Translate the following sentences

(1) According to the international trade practice, unless the buyers require, we usually do not cover these special risks. Your cooperation in this respect would be appreciated.

(2) We regret to inform you that we cannot accept your claim, because you did not cover "Breakage" in the insurance.

(3) If you prefer to effect insurance against All Risks, we would cover it for you. But the premium might be a little higher.

(4) 请按附单所列商品为我方保险。

(5) 保险合同中的所有条款与条件均符合我们要求。

Do You Know

Alternatives to Lying

If you find yourself trapped in an ethical dilemma, find alternatives to lying and thus maintain trust in the negotiations by using these techniques.

(1) When asked what your bottom line is, instead of lying about it, ask your opponents for their bottom line or simply say you are not ready to reveal yours. One negotiator deftly deflects such demands by explaining his goal in the negotiation and assuring his opponent that he will reveal his bottom line in due time.

(2) If you intend to claim "lack of authority" to give up a particular item at the negotiating table, don't seek such authority to do so before the negotiations begin. So when asked, you can truthfully say you do not have the authority or you can even indicate that you do not have the authority but that you will seek it if it means an item can be agreed upon.

(3) If you don't want to volunteer available alternatives to a demand by your opponent because many of those alternatives may provide more than your opponent is actually hoping for, don't say there aren't any when you know there are. Rather, try to elicit your opponent's op-

tions, to which you can respond.

(4) Don't lie about your intentions; only make promises you can keep.

(5) Never lie about facts, focus on the uncertainty of certain facts, or limit your discussion to an expression of your opinion about facts.

(G Richard Shell. Bargaining With the Devil Without Losing Your Soul: Ethics in Negotiation[M]//Carrie Menkel-Meadow, Michael Wheeler. What's Fair: Ethics for Negotiators. San Francisco: Jossey-Bass, 2004.)

Chapter 10 Negotiations on Shipment

第 10 章 装运的谈判

Lead-in

The transportation to be selected depends on the quantity, the cost and the size of each shipment, the distance of transportation, and the nature of goods. Goods can be shipped by surface (road, rail or sea) or by air.

Learning Objectives

In this chapter, you will be able to:

- Know about the negotiations on shipment.
- Know about the strategy of negotiations on shipment.

In international trade, ocean freight is the most widely used form of transportation.[1] It has the attraction of being a cheap mode of transport for delivering large quantities of goods over long distances[2].

Air transport serves as an occasional option.[3] It offers the fastest service, and less packaging is required, but is restrictive on weight and volume, and can be the most expensive method of sending goods[4]. Insurance tends to be cheaper as consignments spend less time in transit.[5]

Fragile and expensive items such as watches and art works are often shipped by air. [6]

Road transport tends to be comparatively cheaper and more direct than rail when transporting relatively small consignments, and offers a door-to-door service, because of the increased capacity for lorries to carry goods, particularly with the introduction of containers, and accessibility abroad with ferries offering rolling-on and rolling-off facilities. [7]

Rail transport is faster than road and can haul bulk goods in greater volume. [8]

Types of vessels are as follows.

About two thirds of the goods are transported by ocean freight in international trade. There are a variety of vessels available for exporters to use when shipping goods. [9]

Passenger liners are ships that follow scheduled routes and concentrate on passenger services, but also carry cargo. [10]

Passenger cargo vessels concentrate on cargoes, offer more facilities for loading and unloading, but carry few passengers. [11]

Tramps travel anywhere in the world on unscheduled routes, picking up any cargo and delivering it. [12]

Tankers are usually oil carriers, and are like bulk carriers which transport bulk consignments such as grain, wheat, and ores. [13]

Container vessels can hold most cargoes including liquids, and are transported by lorries or trains to ports where they are loaded on to container vessels and shipped. [14]

Chartered vessels can be hired to transport products for a particular purpose or time. They can usually be justified for a large order. [15]

Roll-on-roll-off ships are vessels which allow trucks to drive on at one port and off at another without having to load and unload their freight. [16]

There are also barges, large flat-bottomed boats, which transport goods inland along canals and waterways, and lighters which may do that work as a barge, or are used for taking goods from a port out to a ship, or vice versa. [17]

Notes

(1) ocean freight is the most widely used form of transportation.

海洋运输是使用最广泛的运输方式。

(2) It has the attraction of being a cheap mode of transport for delivering large quantities of goods over long distances.

其优点在于价格低、运量大、航程远。

(3) Air transport serves as an occasional option.

航空运输可作为一种供选择的运输方式。

(4) It offers the fastest service, and less packaging is required, but is restrictive on weight and volume, and can be the most expensive method of sending goods.

它提供最快捷的服务,包装要求较低但受重量和体积的限制,属于费用十分昂贵的运输方式。

(5) Insurance tends to be cheaper as consignments spend less time in transit.

保险费较低,运输时间短。

(6) Fragile and expensive items such as watches and art works are often shipped by air.

易碎物品和贵重物品,例如高级手表和工艺品通常采用航空运输。

(7) Road transport tends to be comparatively cheaper and more direct than rail when transporting relatively small consignments, and offers a door-to-door service, because of the increased capacity for lorries to carry goods, particularly with the introduction of containers, and accessibility abroad with ferries offering rolling-on and rolling-off facilities.

运载小批量的货物,公路运输的费用比铁路运输的费用低,且可以直接运进运出货物。由于货车的运载量不断加大,特别是运输中广泛使用集装箱、滚装滚卸船等现代化工具,公路运输还可以提供“门到门”服务。

(8) Rail transport is faster than road and can haul bulk goods in greater volume.

铁道运输比公路运输更快、货运量更大。

(9) About two thirds of the goods are transported by ocean freight in international trade. There are a variety of vessels available for exporters to use when shipping goods.

三分之二的货物是利用海运方式运输的,有可供商家选择的多种海运工具。

(10) Passenger liners are ships that follow scheduled routes and concentrate on passenger services, but also carry cargo.

客船班轮按既定航线进行客运,同时也运载部分货物。

(11) Passenger cargo vessels concentrate on cargoes, offer more facilities for loading and unloading, but carry few passengers.

货船班轮主要用于货运,为装卸货物提供更多便利,很少用于客运。

(12) Tramps travel anywhere in the world on unscheduled routes, picking up any cargo and delivering it.

在世界各地航行的不定期船没有预定的船期表, 船舶经由航线和停靠的港口也不固定。

(13) Tankers are usually oil carriers, and are like bulk carriers which transport bulk consignments such as grain, wheat, and ores.

液体货船通常用于运载石油,或运输像谷类、小麦、矿石等散装货物。

(14) Container vessels can hold most cargoes including liquids, and are transported by lorries or trains to ports where they are loaded on to container vessels and shipped.

集装箱货轮能够运载包括液体在内的各种货物，卡车或火车把集装箱直接运往港口码头，然后在码头把集装箱装上集装箱货轮。

(15) Chartered vessels can be hired to transport products for a particular purpose or time. They can usually be justified for a large order.

包船、租船用于特定的时间内承运指定的货物，通常适用于大宗货物的运输。

(16) Roll-on-roll-off ships are vessels which allow trucks to drive on at one port and off at another without having to load and unload their freight.

滚装滚卸船可以让集装箱卡车直接驶入船内，船到达目的港后，原车即可开上码头，无须在码头上装卸货物。

(17) There are also barges, large flat-bottomed boats, which transport goods inland along canals and waterways, and lighters which may do that work as a barge, or are used for taking goods from a port out to a ship, or vice versa.

此外，驳船和平底船适用于由陆地运河及水路航运的货物运输。驳船也可用于码头与货物之间的驳运。

Traps to Avoid

When You Shouldn't Negotiate

There are many times when you should avoid negotiating. In these situations, stand your ground and you'll come out ahead.

When you'd lose the farm:

If you're in a situation where you could lose everything, choose other options rather than negotiating.

When you're sold out:

When you're running at capacity, don't deal. Raise your price instead.

When the demands are unethical:

Don't negotiate if your counterpart asks for something you cannot support because it's illegal, unethical, or morally inappropriate. When your character or your reputation is compromised, you lose in the long run.

When you don't care:

If you have no stake in the outcome, don't negotiate. You have everything to lose and nothing to gain.

When you don't have time:

When you're pressed for time, you may choose not to negotiate. If the time pressure works against you, you'll make mistakes, and you may fail to consider the implications of your concessions. When under the gun, you'll settle for less than you could otherwise get.

When they act in bad faith:

Stop the negotiation when your counterpart shows signs of acting in bad faith. If you can't trust their negotiating, you can't trust their agreement. In this case negotiation is of little or no value. Stick to your guns and cover your position, or discredit them.

When waiting would improve your position:

Perhaps you'll have a new technology available soon. Maybe your financial situation will improve. Another opportunity may present itself. If the odds are good that you'll gain ground with a delay, wait.

When you're not prepared:

If you don't prepare, you'll think of all your best questions, responses and concessions on the way home. Gathering your reconnaissance and rehearsing the negotiation will pay off handsomely. If you're not ready, just say "no".

(J C Levinson, M S A Smith, O R Wilson. Guerrilla Negotiating: Unconventional Weapons and Tactics to Get What You Want[M]. New York: John Wiley, 1999:22-23.)

Negotiation Examples

1

A: How about the delivery of my goods?[1]

B: Your goods will be first shipped to H. K. in a container ship, and then transshipped to Boston, of course, in another container ship.[2]

A: What if my cargo is less than a container load?[3]

B: Then the cargo will be held at the container freight station until there is a full container load for shipment.

A: It will take time, won't it? And I am worried about ...

B: Don't worry. It wouldn't take much time. We will pay more attention to that, and be sure you can get the goods on time.

A: How do you know when my goods will be ready to leave your country?

B: We will keep in touch with the shipping company all the time. We have close business relations with them.

A：Are the containers temperature-controlled?[4]

B：Yes. They are also watertight and airtight to protect goods from being damaged by heat, water or dampness.[5] The containers can be opened at both ends, so that loading and unloading can be made at the same time.[6]

A：Containerization is faster, safer and more convenient.[7] It can also save a lot of wrapping and the cost of freight.[8]

B：I think containerization is one of the best methods in the transportation of goods.[9]

Notes

(1) How about the delivery of my goods?

我方货物的运输怎样安排?

(2) Your goods will be first shipped to H. K. in a container ship, and then transshipped to Boston, of course, in another container ship.

你方货物先用集装箱运往香港,然后再在香港转船运往波士顿。

(3) What if my cargo is less than a container load?

如果我的货物不满一个集装箱怎么办?

(4) Are the containers temperature-controlled?

集装箱是恒温的吗?

(5) They are also watertight and airtight to protect goods from being damaged by heat, water or dampness.

同时集装箱还防水、密封,货物不会受热、受潮。

(6) The containers can be opened at both ends, so that loading and unloading can be made at the same time.

集装箱两端都能打开,所以能同时装货、卸货。

(7) Containerization is faster, safer and more convenient.

集装箱运输更快、更安全、更便利。

(8) It can also save a lot of wrapping and the cost of freight.

还可以省下一笔包装费和运输费。

(9) I think containerization is one of the best methods in the transportation of goods.

我认为集装箱运输是最好的货物运输工具之一。

2

A：Could you do something to advance your time of shipment[1]?

B：Well, our manufacturers are fully committed at the moment[2]. I'm afraid it's very difficult to improve any further on the time.

A: I hope you'll try to get them round to step up production[3].

B: We check their production schedule against our orders almost every day[4]. As new orders keep coming in, and they are working three shifts to step up production[5]. I'm sorry, but we simply cannot commit ourselves beyond what the production schedule can fulfill[6].

A: Well, in that case, there is nothing more to be said. What's your last word as to the date then?

B: I said by the middle of September. This is the best we can promise.

A: All right. I'll take you at your word. May I suggest that you put down in the contract "shipment on September 20 or earlier?" Our letter of credit will be opened in early August.

B: Good. Let's call it a deal[7]. We'll do our best to advance the shipment to August. The chances are that some of the other orders may be cancelled. But of course you cannot count on that. In any case, we'll let you know by cable.

A: That's very considerate of you. And now, shall we discuss the insurance term?

B: OK. We generally insure W. A. on a C. I. F. offer.

Notes

(1) Could you do something to advance your time of shipment?
您可否想办法提前装船时间?

(2) Our manufacturers are fully committed at the moment.
我们的生产商订货已满。

(3) I hope you'll try to get them round to step up production.
我希望你们能尽力说服他们提高产量。

(4) We check their production schedule against our orders almost every day.
我们几乎每天都查对他们的生产计划,以了解我们订单的完成情况。

(5) New orders keep coming in, and they are working three shifts to step up production.
新的订单不断,他们为了提高产量进行三班倒。

(6) We simply cannot commit ourselves beyond what the production schedule can fulfill.
生产计划以外能完成多少,我们真的无法承诺。

(7) Let's call it a deal.
这笔交易就敲定吧。

Word Bank

deliver sth. to sb./to make delivery 发货

port of delivery　发货港
shipping space　舱位
direct steamer　直达轮
to urge/expedite shipment　催促、加速装船
punctual shipment/delivery　按时装船
shipping instruction　装船须知
shipping mark　装运标志
shipping order　装货单
time of shipment　装船期
immediate shipments　立即装运
prompt shipments　即期装运
express shipment　即期装运
to delay shipment　延期装运
to effect shipment　装运
to hasten shipment/to speed up shipment　加速装运
transshipment　转船
transshipment permitted　允许转运
transshipment on route　中途转运
initial shipment　第一批货
transshipment charges　转运费
transshipment entry　转运报单
transshipment manifest　转运舱单
discharging/load off/unloading　卸货
loading rate　装船率
air waybill　航空运单
combined transport documents　多式联运单据
shipper, consignor　托运人(一般指出口商)
regular shipping liner　班轮
lighter　驳船
tanker　油轮
clearance of goods　报关
cargo receipt　陆运收据
to take delivery of goods　提货
airway bill　空运提单
original B/L　正本提单

optional port 选择港(任意港)

optional charges 选港费

optional charges to be borne by the Buyers 或 optional charges for Buyers' account 选港费由买方负担

shipment during Jan./Feb. 或 Jan./Feb. shipment 一/二月份装船

shipment during...in two lots 在……(时间)分两批装船

in three equal monthly shipments 分三个月,每月平均装运

shipments within 30 days after receipt of L/C 收到信用证后30天内装运

partial shipment 分批装船

Useful Sentences

(1) It's essential to choose the right means of transportation.

选择合适的运输方式很重要。

(2) To ensure a faster delivery, you are asked to forward the order by air freight.

为了确保迅速交货,我方要求此订货用空运。

(3) Generally speaking, it's cheaper but slower to ship goods by sea than by rail.

总的来说,海运比铁路运输更便宜,但速度慢一些。

(4) It's faster but more expensive to ship goods by air.

空运较快但运费较高。

(5) Since we need the goods urgently, we must insist on express shipment.

由于我方急需这批货物,我方坚持使用快递装运。

(6) Because of the type of purchase, we can only ship by road.

由于商品的性质,我方只能使用公路运输。

(7) If the customer requests a carrier other than truck, he must bear the additional charge.

如果顾客坚持用卡车以外的运输工具,就必须负担额外费用。

(8) The goods will be transhipped in Hong Kong.

货物将在香港转船。

(9) There may be some quantity difference when loading the goods, but not more than 5%.

货物装船时可能会有一些数量出入,但不会超过5%。

(10) To make it easier for us to get the goods ready for shipment, we hope that partial shipment is allowed.

为了便于我方备货装船,希望允许分批发运。

(11) The delivery has to be put off due to the strike of the workers at the port.

由于港口工人罢工,交货只好推迟。

(12) We are sorry to delay the shipment because our manufacturer has met unexpected difficulties.

恕延期货船,因为我们厂家遇到了预料不到的困难。

(13) We assume that damage occurred while the consignment was in your care.

我们认为货物是在你方保管时受到损害的。

(14) The consignment appears to have been roughly handled and left near a heater.

看来货物未受到细心的处理,并且被放置于加热器附近。

(15) I'm afraid I have some rather bad news for you.

我恐怕有些很坏的消息要告诉你。

Tactics for Success

How to Choose the Means of Transportation

There are many means of transportation. Trains are usually used to transport heavy or bulky products that are low in value, such as lumber, coal or chemicals. One of the most important advantages of railroad transportation is that it is seldom affected by weather.

Truck is a convenient and profitable mode of transportation for short-distance shipment because it can stop within a city and deliver goods directly to the markets. Trucks are not limited to any fixed schedules, as the trains and airplanes are. They can pick up or deliver a small or a large shipment anywhere at any time.

Air freight is a quick means of transportation. When speed is taken into consideration, this means will be most effective owing to its swift delivery. Some valuable goods like furs, silks, art goods, fresh flowers and fashionable articles that have a short selling life are usually transported by air freight.

Pipelines is a special type of transportation used mainly to transport certain products like gasoline, crude oil, natural gas, and so on.

In China and most other countries, ocean freight is generally regarded as a cheap mode of transportation for delivering large quantities of goods over long distance. In spite of its disadvantages of being slow and affected by weather conditions, about two thirds of the goods are transported by ocean freight in international trade. In China almost 80% of our imported and exported goods are handled through sea ports.

(浩瀚. 商务英语谈判实例实战[M]. 北京: 中国水利水电出版社, 2009: 145.)

Exercises

Ⅰ. Translate the following words and phrases

shipping agent
shipping company
partial shipment
to advance shipment
in bulk
vessel
commercial invoice
liner
shipping marks
prompt delivery
装船条款
运输方式
发货时间
装船通知
海关申报单
装箱单
集装箱、货柜
提货单
装船费
装船单

Ⅱ. Translate the following sentences

(1) As soon as shipping space is booked, we shall inform you of the name of the ship.

(2) The cargo will be held according to ports of discharge and nature of cargo at the container freight.

(3) The containers are also watertight and airtight to protect goods from being damaged by heat, water or dampness.

(4) 集装箱两端都能打开,所以能同时装货、卸货。

(5) 集装箱运输更快、更安全、更便利,还可以省下一笔包装费和运输费。

Do You Know

Differences among Negotiators

Differences can be the barrier to reaching agreement. Negotiators must learn to manage conflict effectively in order to manage their differences while searching for ways to maximize their joint value.

Differences in interests(利益的不同). Negotiators seldom value all items in a negotiation equally. For example, in discussing a compensation package, a company may be more willing to concede on a signing bonus than on salary because the bonus occurs only in the first year, while salary is a permanent expense. An advertising company may be quite willing to bend on creative control of a project, but very protective of control over advertising placement. Finding compatibility in different interests is often the key to unlocking the puzzle of value creation.

Differences in judgments about the future(对未来判断的不同). People differ in their evaluation of what something is worth or the future value of an item. For instance, is that piece of swamp land a good or bad investment of your hard-earned income? Some people can imagine the future house site and swimming pool, whereas others will see it as a bug-infested flood control problem. Real estate developers work hard to identify properties where they see future potential that current owners fail to recognize.

Differences in risk tolerance(风险承受能力的不同). People differ in the amount of risk they are comfortable assuming. A young, single-income family with three children can sustain less risk than a mature, dual-income couple without children. A company with a cash flow problem can assume less risk of expanding its operations than one that is cash rich.

Differences in time preference(时间偏好的不同). Negotiators frequently differ in how time affects them. One negotiator may want to realize gains now while the other may be happy to defer gains into the future; one needs a quick settlement while the other has no need for any change in the status quo. Differences in time preferences have the potential to create value in a negotiation. For example, a car salesman may want to close a deal by the end of the week in order to be eligible for a special company bonus, while the potential buyer intends to trade his car sometime in the next six months.

(Roy J Lewicki, Bruce Barry, David M Saunders. 谈判学精要[M]. 大连：东北财经大学出版社，2008.)

Chapter 11 Negotiation Strategies
第 11 章 谈判策略

Lead-in

Negotiation strategies are established in order to achieve the negotiation objectives. Therefore, choices of strategy and negotiation techniques are vital. How to deal with difficult people and difficult situations and how to handle conflicts in negotiation will be learned in this chapter.

Learning Objectives

In this chapter, you will be able to:

- Learn choices of strategy.
- Know negotiation strategies.
- Know how to deal with difficult people and situations.

A negotiation only succeeds if the parties "buy into" the agreement and are truly willing to fulfill the bargain they have made. Negotiators should pay attention to such phases as: pre-negotiation, face-to-face negotiation and post-negotiation[1].

Pre-negotiation. The pre-negotiation stage begins from the first contact between the two parties when both show their interest in doing business with each other. It is from this stage that both parties begin to understand one another's demands and evaluate the benefits of entering into the process of negotiation[2]. Both parties now gather as much information as possible on each other, such as the operating environment, involvement of other parties, and even customs and tendencies. And we need keep an open mind to recognize and accept the differences among various cultures[3]. For example, Chinese and American negotiators always hold different opinions about the beginning phase. Chinese are likely to develop good relationship and devote much time to inviting others to dinners and tea, whereas Americans consider it as a waste of time and prefer to go straight to the point.[4]

Face-to-Face Negotiation. The middle phase of negotiation includes the exchange of information and persuasion. What is worth noticing is that an initial discussion on items of common interest helps create an atmosphere of cooperation. At this stage, negotiators should adopt some feasible strategies and proper communication skills to reach an agreement.[5] And we know conflict tends to be more difficult and complex when involved with cultural differences, because methods of communication vary among cultures. But conflict is unavoidable during the process of negotiations. To make things worse, poor communication may spoil deals. Sometimes, negotiators' strategies can be revealed in the content and form of their communication. So we should avoid bringing along own cultural assumptions to the negotiating table, and then try our best to overcome the cultural differences on negotiation, and utilize effective communication to gain the common interest. In view of its significance in negotiation, communication is at the heart of the negotiating process. Measures should be taken to:

Avoid highly personal questions and issues on politics and religion;

Avoid slang, jargons and figurative expressions;[6]

Pronounce words explicitly and speak somewhat slowly;[7]

Provide frequent feedback to determine whether the listeners have understood;

Avoid interrupting the speaker before the message is completed;

Avoid impolite jokes and offending sentences.

In case of disagreement, expressions such as "incomplete, needing adjustment, almost concurring with you but, heading in the same direction" will make the situation better.[8]

It is important to avoid revealing ignorance about the counterpart's information, which is embarrassing and offensive.

Post-negotiation. Finally, the business negotiation is brought to the final stage. All the terms have been agreed on at this stage. The contract is being drawn up and to be signed. However, writing and wording of the contract in itself is a kind of negotiating process. Due to the cultural factors involved in the business negotiation, the form of agreement is different from culture to culture. For example, Americans may prefer the agreement that is an explicit, detailed, written contract that covers all the things that may happen in the future.[9] On the contrary, Chinese people may prefer an implicit, broad contract in the form of general principles rather than detailed rules. [10] So it is productive to confirm that both parties understand everything they have agreed on.

There are many issues which should be taken into consideration regarding negotiation strategies, such as non-verbal communication strategy and haggling strategy.

(1) Non-verbal communication strategy. For the voice, one should breathe slowly and control the volume. As to the speed, one should not speak too fast and pause frequently. In terms of languages, short sentences, examples and summaries are preferred. Sense of humor often helps. Notes are necessary, but not complete texts. As for the eye contact, one should avoid looking away. For the posture, one should sit at a table, wearing a smile and keeping nodding, avoiding scratching the face or nose[11], and dressing in a conventional way.

(2) Haggling strategy. It requires understanding your own motive. Without your bottom line for a particular product, you will quickly fall into the trap of being out-priced, or losing the item to a price you may not have had to pay for. ① Learn to bid very low: This will make sellers stop and reflect about the price, which could be too high or they may overlook something. Whatever the case may be, you can start out by completely undercutting the initial offer, giving you the chance to gauge the sale with accuracy. ② Play the role of inspector: Make sure to touch, feel, and account for any flaws or legitimate defects on the product. This will give you a chance for leverage to secure a lower price easily. ③ Choose your own add-ons: It helps to "seal the deal" by creating additional value. If the seller will not cut the price, you may add another item.

Notes

(1) Negotiators should pay attention to the following phases: pre-negotiation, face-to-face negotiation and post-negotiation.

谈判方应该关注如下三个阶段：谈判前，谈判中和谈判后。

(2) It is from this stage that both parties begin to understand one another's demands and evaluate the benefits of entering into the process of negotiation.

从这个阶段开始，双方开始了解对方的需求，并评估进入谈判过程的优势。

(3) We need keep an open mind to recognize and accept the difference among various cultures.

我们应该视野开阔，意识到并接受不同文化之间的差异。

(4) Americans consider it as a waste of time and prefer to go straight to the point.

美国人认为这是浪费时间，喜欢开门见山。

(5) Negotiators should adopt some feasible strategies and proper communication skills to

reach an agreement.

要达成共识，谈判者应该采取灵活的措施和恰当的交际技能。

(6) Avoid slang, jargons and figurative expressions.

避免使用俚语、行话和修辞类表达。

(7) Pronounce words explicitly and speak somewhat slowly.

明确清晰地说话，语速慢一些。

(8) In case of disagreement, expressions such as "incomplete, needing adjustment, almost concurring with you but, heading in the same direction" will make the situation better.

如果有异议，较好的表达方式有"不太完整、需要调整、基本上同意您但是、我们的方向是一致的"。

(9) Americans may prefer the agreement that is an explicit, detailed, written contract that covers all the things that may happen in the future.

美国人喜欢明确、详细的合同，要包括所有，甚至是未来的事情。

(10) Chinese people may prefer an implicit, broad contract in the form of general principles rather than detailed rules.

中国人喜欢概括的合同，以宽泛代替详细的风格。

(11) Avoid scratching the face or nose.

避免用手搓脸或鼻子。

Traps to Avoid

Wait to Counter

After receiving the opening offer from the other party—or in fact any offer—a good tactic is to wait before responding. Why? A response delivered too quickly may cause the other party to think you did not seriously consider the merits of their offer, and may even appear that you are belittling them. Waiting a respectful amount of time to respond, even if you never had any intention of accepting their offer, will make your opponent feel better about the process. After waiting a respectful period of time, you can reject the offer, or even better, respond with "We have considered your offer and would like to propose that you consider this counteroffer..." This tactic of waiting to respond to an offer shows a level of respect for the other party—and can help both parties reach an agreement.

(Michael R Carrell, Christina Heavrin. The Everyday Negotiator[M]. Amherst: HRD Press, 2004: 99-102.)

Negotiation Examples

1

A: Mr. Smith, last time I failed in the negotiation. One of our colleagues tells me that I should pay attention to the use of non-verbal communication.[1] Do you have any other suggestions to me?

B: Well, when you sit, you may keep your back straight so as to show respect to your counterpart.[2] Meanwhile, wear a smile. Smile can work as a diplomat as negotiation needs concession and cooperation.[3]

A: My friends tell me to make a list of questions. I have prepared four questions. What is the purpose of opening the negotiation with this particular group?[4] What is our main goal in the target market? Is it trade or investment? What level of agenda control can we expect?

B: Good. Other questions like "Is this a buying or selling position? What level of experience does our team or do I have in negotiations of this type? What are the issues to be negotiated? What issues are considered to be needed for our position?" Another factor you should bear in mind is that you cannot appear too needy, which could make the deal unattractive even before it is on the table.[5] Conversely, approaching a deal in a take-or-leave-it manner may only attract the most desperate partners, or none at all.[6]

A: To sum up, to achieve a successful negotiation, one needs thorough reflection on the related questions. Once the answers have been given, rethink the guidelines from the opposition's point of view.

B: Yes. I agree with that. Understanding the other party greatly reduces risk.[7] Tomorrow, I will give a lecture on the offensive and defensive tactics, if you have time, you may come to share ideas with us.

Notes

(1) One of our colleagues tells me that I should pay attention to the use of non-verbal communication.

我的一位同事告诉我应该注意非语言交际手段。

(2) Keep your back straight so as to show respect to your counterpart.

要挺直后背,这样表示对对方的尊重。

(3) Meanwhile, wear a smile. Smile can work as a diplomat as negotiation needs concession and cooperation.

同时，要保持微笑。微笑可以是一种外交手段，因为谈判需要让步和合作。

(4) What is the purpose of opening the negotiation with this particular group?

和这个公司开始谈判的目的是什么？

(5) Another factor you should bear in mind is that you cannot appear too needy, which could make the deal unattractive even before it is on the table.

另一个因素是您要记住，不能显示出太急，那样会使得谈判还没开始就显得没有吸引力了。

(6) Conversely, approaching a deal in a take-or-leave-it manner may only attract the most desperate partners, or none at all.

相反，要以一种淡定的态度进行谈判，这样可能吸引很迫切的合作者，当然也可能得到相反的结果。

(7) Understanding the other side greatly reduces risk.

了解对方会大大地减少风险。

2

A: Hi, everyone. Let's clap our hands to welcome Mr. Zhao to our company. This is a precious chance for us to invite him to give us some ideas on negotiation strategies. He is an excellent negotiator and will share with us his experience.

B: Hello, everyone. It is my greatest honor to be here today. Generally speaking, there are three stages in you negotiation. At each stage, we should be prepared fully so that we can achieve success finally.

A: What stages are they?

B: They are pre-negotiation stage, face-to-face negotiation stage and post-negotiation stage. [1] A particular stage ends where the parties decide to proceed further on to the next stage or decide to abandon the communication if they see no point in further negotiations. [2]

A: During the pre-negotiation stage, tentative offers are made. You should be aware that the relationship can be altered at any time by such events as the repositioning of competitors or movements in exchange rates. [3]

B: That means, both parties should define problems jointly.

A: Exactly. It can reflect both parties' expectations and commitments. [4] So the parties should truly and openly discuss each other's objectives in order to achieve a positive problem-solving situation. [5]

B: We may have informal meetings to know more about each other's expectations.

A: Yes. The first strategy is to keep your communication simple and straightforward. [6] Do not use any slang or jargons.

B: Some people say that the best negotiators create "win-win" situations in every negotiation.

A: Sure, the second strategy is that negotiation is not an "I win, you lose" condition[7]. But you cannot let your counterpart know what you desire most, otherwise your position is not strong enough. The third one is to pretend to appear to be surprised. After the other party presents the offer, you need to let them feel uncomfortable. You must appear shocked and surprised that the supplier be bold enough to request such a high figure[8]. Your counterpart may offer an immediate concession.

B: This is a good strategy. We can also use this way to ask for discounts from the suppliers.

A: This is the fourth strategy. As a consumer, you should form the habit of asking for a price break when you buy from a retail store. Be pleasant and persistent, but not demanding and aggressive. Conditioning yourself to negotiate at every chance will help you become more comfortable and ready when the time comes to negotiate for your business.

Notes

(1) They are pre-negotiation stage, face-to-face negotiation stage and post-negotiation stage.

他们分别是谈判前、谈判中和谈判后阶段。

(2) A particular stage ends where the parties decide to proceed further on to the next stage or decide to abandon the communication if they see no point in further negotiations.

当谈判的一个阶段结束时,双方决定进入到下一个阶段或者由于没有进展而放弃合作。

(3) You should be aware that the relationship can be altered at any time by such events as the repositioning of competitors or movements in exchange rates.

您应该意识到当竞争者移位或汇率有变化时,双方的关系都可能因此发生变化。

(4) It can reflect both parties' expectations and commitments.

它会反映双方的期望和承诺。

(5) So the parties should truly and openly discuss each other's objectives in order to achieve a positive problem-solving situation.

双方应该真诚而公开地讨论彼此的目标来达到积极解决问题的状态。

(6) The first strategy is to keep your communication simple and straightforward.

第一个策略就是交流时要简单直接。

(7) The second strategy is not to make the negotiation an "I win, you lose" condition.

第二个策略就是不要把谈判搞成"我赢你输"的情形。

(8) You must appear shocked and surprised that the supplier be bold enough to request such a high figure.

得知供应商胆敢要这样高的价格,您必须显得很吃惊的样子。

Word Bank

force majeure 不可抗力
arbitral tribunal 仲裁庭
certificate of origin 产地证明书
inspection certificate of quality 品质检验证书
inspection certificate of weight (quantity) 重量检验证书
commodity inspection bureau (C. I. B) 商品检验局
inspection certificate 品质、重量检验证书
foreign exchange 外汇
devaluation 贬值
foreign currency 外币
revaluation 升值
rate of exchange 汇率
floating rate 浮动汇率
balance of payments 国际收支差额,贸易收支差额
hard currency 硬通货
fair average quality 大路货(良好平均品质)
direct quotation 直接标价
soft currency 软通货
indirect quotation 间接标价
buying rate 买入汇率
inflation 通货膨胀
selling rate 卖出汇率
fixed rate 固定汇率
gold standard 金本位
gold points 黄金输送点
mint par 铸币平价
paper money system 纸币制度
international monetary fund 国际货币基金
gold and foreign exchange reserve 黄金外汇储备

official upper and lower limits of fluctuation 汇率波动的官定上下限

Useful Sentences

(1) We are really glad to see your suggestion so constructive in helping settle the problems as regards the signing of the contract.

我们很高兴您提出很多有建设性的意见,解决了很多问题。

(2) Here are the two originals of the contract we prepared.

这是我们准备好的两份合同正本。

(3) Would you please read the draft contract and make your comments about the terms?

请仔细阅读合同草案,并就合同各条款提出你的看法好吗?

(4) We have compensation trade and joint venture.

我们有补偿贸易和合资经营。

(5) We are always willing to cooperate with you and if necessary make some concessions.

我们总是愿意合作的,如果需要还可以做些让步。

(6) I think you probably know China has adopted a flexible policy in her foreign trade.

我想你也许已经了解到中国在对外贸易中采取了灵活的政策。

(7) We'd like to clear up some points connected with the technical part of the contract.

我们希望搞清楚有关合同中技术方面的几个问题。

(8) The negotiations on the rights and obligations of the parties under contract turned out to be very successful.

就合同各方的权利和义务方面的谈判非常成功。

(9) The loss for this should be charged to the party breaking the contract.

造成的损失必须由毁约方承担。

(10) Do not personalize the situation or the behavior of the other party, because you should realize that their behavior is not a personal attack on you personally.

不要以个人的角度看待谈判当时的情景和对方的行为,因为它们不是针对你个人的攻击行为。

(11) Additional items can be addressed in subsequent negotiations.

其他条款会在以后的谈判中协商。

(12) Some of the negotiators are hard to deal with. Because they have rigid thinking pattern and are unwilling to compromise. What is worse is that they tend to pursue win-lose outcomes.

有些谈判者很难缠,因为他们的思维固化,而且不愿意妥协。更糟糕的是,他们只在乎成败。

(13) When both parties have a sense of urgency, it is easier to reach an agreement.

当谈判双方都有紧迫感时，才更容易达成一致。

(14) The two parties need to express willingness to settle disagreement.

谈判双方需要表达解决分歧的意愿。

(15) Some of the settlements may be substantively acceptable but may be impossible to implement.

有些解决方法可以接受但却不可行。

Tactics for Success

Effective Conflict Management

The Dual Concerns Model

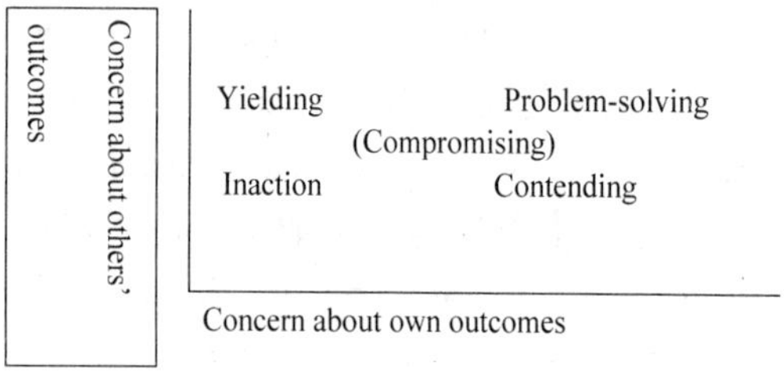

(J Rubin, D Pruitt, S H Kim. Social Conflict: Escalation, Stalemate and Settlement[M]. 2nd ed. New York: McGraw-Hill, 1994.)

Styles of Handling Interpersonal Conflict and Situations Where They Are Appropriate or Inappropriate

Conflict Style	Situations Where Appropriate	Situations Where Inappropriate
Integrating (collaborating, Problem solving): Show high concern for attaining his own outcomes and high concern for whether the other party attains his outcomes	(1) Issues are complex. (2) Synthesis of ideas is needed to come up with better solutions. (3) Commitment is needed from other parties for successful implementation. (4) Time is available for problem solving. (5) One party alone cannot solve the problem. (6) Resources possessed by different parties are needed to solve their common problems	(1) Task or problem is simple. (2) Immediate decision is required. (3) Other parties are unconcerned about outcome. (4) Other parties do not have problem-solving skills

续表

Conflict Style	Situations Where Appropriate	Situations Where Inappropriate
Obliging(Yielding, Accommodating): Show little interest or concern in whether he attain his own outcomes, but he is interested in whether the other party attains his outcomes	(1) You believe you may be wrong. (2) Issue is more important to the other party. (3) You are willing to give up something in exchange for something from the other party in the future. (4) You are dealing from a position of weakness. (5) Preserving relationship is important	(1) Issue is important to you. (2) You believe you are right. (3) The other party is wrong or unethical
Dominating(Competing, Contending): Pursue his own outcomes strongly and show little concern for whether the other party obtains his desired outcomes	(1) Issue is trivial. (2) Speedy decision is needed. (3) Unpopular course of action is implemented. (4) Necessary to overcome assertive subordinates. (5) Unfavorable decision by the other party may be costly to you. (6) Subordinates lack expertise to make technical decisions. (7) Issue is important to you	(1) Issue is complex. (2) Issue is not important to you. (3) Both parties are equally powerful. (4) Decision does not have to be made quickly. (5) Subordinates possess high degree of competence
Avoiding(Inaction): Show little interest in whether he attains his own outcomes, as well as little concern about whether the other party obtains his outcomes	(1) Issue is trivial. (2) Potential dysfunctional effect of confronting the other party outweighs benefits of resolution. (3) Cooling off period is needed	(1) Issue is important to you. (2) It is your responsibility to make a decision. (3) Parties are unwilling to defer; issue must be resolved. (4) Prompt attention is needed
Compromising: A moderate effort to pursue one's own outcomes and a moderate effort to help the other party to achieve his outcomes	(1) Goals of parties are mutually exclusive. (2) Parties are equally powerful. (3) Consensus cannot be reached. (4) Integrating or dominating style is not successful. (5) Temporary solution to a complex problem I needed	(1) One party is more powerful. (2) Problem is complex enough to need a problem-solving approach

(M A Rahim. Rahim Organizational Conflict Inventories: Professional Manual[M]. Mountain View: Consulting Psychologists Press, 1990.)

Exercises

Ⅰ. Translate the following words and phrases

duplicate sample
original sample
counter sample
standard type
sealed sample
pamphlet
sample
assortment
5% plus or minus
representative sample
品质
规格
说明
参考样品
商品目录
索赔
争议
罚金条款
仲裁
货号

Ⅱ. Translate the following sentences

(1) Today's lecture is on how to deal with difficult people and difficult situations.

(2) Conflicts can be stimulating, such as competition, and will contribute to the overall goodness of all parties involved.

(3) In negotiation, we must try our utmost to minimize losses and maximize gains.

(4) 了解某公司的核心价值和出其不意是谈判的两个重要策略。

(5) 处理谈判冲突,最重要的是要先创造一个轻松的氛围。

Do You Know

Common Nonverbal Behaviors

May indicate can be trusted	May indicate dishonesty	May indicate closed-mindedness	May indicate willingness to listen
direct speech; open gestures; open behavior; smiling; pointing	fidgeting; excessive smiling; sheepish smiles; overly serious tone; lack of emotion; averting eyes; lack of eye contact; being too quiet	using briefcase or papers to "guard" body; crossing arms; turning body away	leaning forward in seat; keeping arms and palms open; maintain great eye contact; nodding

(Michael R Carrell, Christina Heavrin. Negotiating Essentials: Theory, Skills and Practices[M]. Upper Saddle River: Prentice Hall, 2010: 127.)

参 考 文 献

[1] 张立玉,陈珞瑜. 商务英语谈判[M]. 北京:高等教育出版社,2011.

[2] 诸葛霖. 外贸英语对话[M]. 北京:对外经济贸易大学出版社,1998.

[3] 肖云南,全英,陈勇. 国际商务谈判[M]. 北京:北方交通大学出版社,2003.

[4] 浩瀚. 商务英语谈判900句典[M]. 北京:机械工业出版社,2008.

[5] 浩瀚. 国际贸易英语实例实战[M]. 北京:中国水利水电出版社,2010.

[6] 朱文忠,周杏英. 实用商务谈判英语[M]. 北京:对外经济贸易大学出版社, 2007.

[7] 廖瑛. 实用外贸谈判英语教程 [M]. 北京:对外经济贸易大学出版社, 2010.

[8] 丁衡祁,张静. 商务谈判英语[M]. 北京:对外经济贸易大学出版社, 2009.

[9] 张立玉,邓之宇,石定乐. 商务谈判英语[M]. 武汉:武汉大学出版社, 2009.

[10] http://huihua. iciba. com.

[11] http://hr. wtojob. com.

[12] http://chinese. mercialleasing. com.

[13] http://www. iciba. com.

[14] http://www. newuxi. com.

[15] http://iask. sina. com. cn.

[16] http://chinese. nnkl. com.

[17] http://my. iciba. com.

[18] http://www. 24en. com.

[19] http://www. lw23. com.

[20] http://www. haoqiantu. cn.

[21] http://kafeidou003402. blog. 163. com.

[22] http://www. study-abroad-web. com.

[23] http://www. lw23. com.

[24] http://blog. 163. com.

[25] http://www. zzer. org.

[26] http://learning. sohu. com.

[27] http://qd. haagee. com.

[28] http://sesepingfeng. bokee. com.

[29] http://www. jobe23. com.

[30] http://247974785. qzone. qq. com.

[31] http://jukuu. com.

[32] http://www. dshrc. com.

[33] http://jobcomcnold. jobcomcn. com.

[34] http://www. chinaenglish. com. cn/html/c108/2009-11/36387. html.

[35] http://article. yeeyan. org.

[36] http://goabroad. wenda. sogou. com.